Good Housekeeping

COMPLETE BOOK
OF PASTA

Good Housekeeping
COMPLETE BOOK OF PASTA

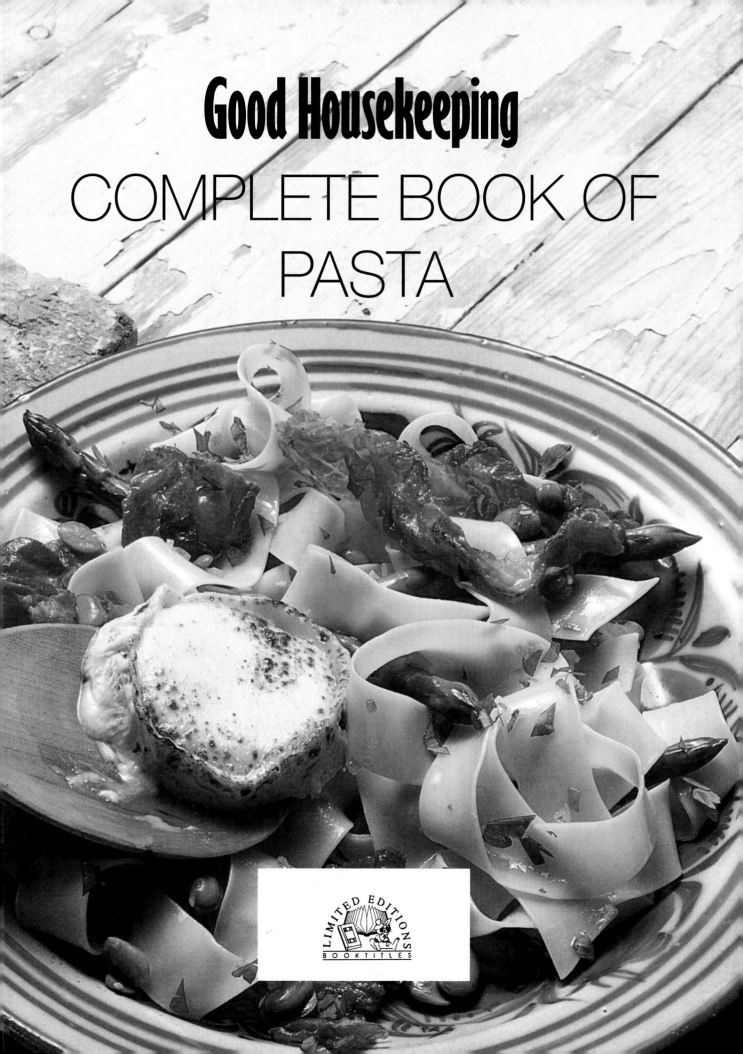

LIMITED EDITIONS
BOOKTITLES

This edition published by Limited Editions in 1996

1 3 5 7 9 10 8 6 4 2

First published in the United Kingdom in 1996 by Ebury Press, Random House, 20 Vauxhall Bridge Road, London SW1V 2SA

Random House Australia (Pty) Limited
20 Alfred Street, Milsons Point, Sydney,
New South Wales 2061, Australia

Random House New Zealand Limited
18 Poland Road, Glenfield,
Auckland 10, New Zealand

Random House South Africa (Pty) Limited
PO Box 337, Bergvlei, South Africa

Random House UK Limited Reg. No. 954009

A CIP catalogue record for this book is available from the British Library.

Managing Editor: JANET ILLSLEY
Design: CHRISTINE WOOD
Special Photography: GRAHAM KIRK
Food Stylist: LOUISE PICKFORD
Photographic Stylist: HELEN PAYNE
Recipe Testing: EMMA-LEE GOW
Illustrations: DAVID DOWNTON

Contributing Authors: LOUISE PICKFORD, LYN RUTHERFORD, MAXINE CLARK, CAROLINE YATES, JOANNA FARROW, JACQUELINE CLARKE, JANET SMITH

Other photographs: KEN FIELD, pages 48 and 116; GUS FILGATE, page 146; JAMES MURPHY, page 150

ISBN 0 09 185 751 1

Typeset in Helvetica

Colour reproduction by Colorlito Rigogliosi s.r.l., Milan

Printed and bound in Portugal by Printer Portuguesa L.d.a.

COOKERY NOTES

- Both metric and imperial measures are given for the recipes. Follow either metric or imperial throughout as they are not interchangeable.

- All spoon measures are level unless otherwise stated. Sets of measuring spoons are available in metric and imperial for accurate measurement of small quantities.

- Ovens should be preheated to the specified temperature. Grills should also be preheated. The cooking times given in the recipes assume that this has been done.

- Unless otherwise suggested at the end of the recipe, the dish is not suitable for freezing.

- Use size 2 eggs except where otherwise specified. Free-range eggs are recommended.

- Use freshly ground black pepper and sea salt unless otherwise specified.

- Use fresh rather than dried herbs unless dried herbs are suggested in the recipe.

- Stocks should be freshly made if possible. Alternatively buy ready-made stocks or use good quality stock cubes.

CONTENTS

INTRODUCTION

In Italy, hardly a meal is served without pasta and elsewhere in the world pasta has become incredibly popular. It is – after all – inexpensive, quick to cook and extremely versatile. The range of dried and fresh pastas readily available from supermarkets and delicatessens today is seemingly endless and, of course, you can combine these with all manner of tasty sauces.

From a nutritional angle, pasta is essentially a carbohydrate food but, because it has a low fat content, pasta isn't particularly high in calories. It's the accompanying sauces that make the recipes fattening; so if you are watching your weight, use low-calorie ingredients, such as vegetables, skimmed milk and low-fat cheese to replace full-fat ingredients, and keep the use of ingredients like olive oil, butter and olives to a minimum. Some varieties of pasta, notably those made with eggs, contain as much as 13 per cent protein, as well as useful vitamins and minerals.

HOMEMADE PASTA
Although the availability of commercial fresh pastas is ever-increasing, there is no real substitute for homemade pasta. It is surprisingly quick and rewarding to make, and has a wonderfully light texture and incomparable flavour – almost melting in the mouth. If you have never attempted to make your own pasta, do give it a try, using the recipe on page 10.

You need very little basic equipment – a rolling pin, metal pastry cutters, a sharp knife and a pastry wheel will suffice – but, if you intend to make pasta regularly, invest in a pasta machine to take all of the hard work out of rolling and cutting. A pasta machine will also ensure that the dough is even and very thin, giving excellent results.

Once you have mastered the basic recipe, try your hand at some of the flavoured pastas – they are just as easy and quite delicious.

BOUGHT FRESH PASTA
Many supermarkets and Italian delicatessens now sell fresh pasta. If you prefer to buy fresh pasta rather than make your own or use dried, it is worth searching out a good supplier. Commercially produced fresh pasta tends to be unpleasantly thick and stodgy – quite unlike homemade pasta. However, Italian delicatessens often sell good quality pasta which has been freshly prepared on the premises, in an interesting range of flavours.

DRIED PASTA
Dried pasta is available in an extensive range of shapes, sizes and flavours. The best are made from 100% durum wheat (*pasta di semola grano duro*); some include eggs (*all'uova*). With the exception of filled pastas, such as ravioli, dried pasta is suitable for all of the recipes in this book.

The variety of dried pasta shapes is almost bewildering. The names of shapes often vary from one region of Italy to another, and new ones are constantly being introduced. Below is a guide to the most common types, but this list is not exhaustive. You will also find a selection of dried pasta illustrated overleaf, and identified on page 11 for reference. Note that the suffix gives an indication of the size of the pasta. *Oni* denotes large, as in *conchiglioni* (large shells); -*ette* or -*etti* suggests small, as in *spaghetti* and *cappelletti* (small hats); while -*ine* or -*ini* means tiny, as in *stellette* (tiny soup pasta).

COMMON PASTA SHAPES
Spaghetti: Long, thin straight strands, available in slightly differing thicknesses. *Spaghettini* is a finer version of spaghetti; *lingiune* is very slightly thicker. *Bucatini* is a thicker version.

Macaroni: Thicker tubular pasta, available in long and short lengths, often slightly curved, sometimes ridged. Short kinds include *penne*, *tubetti* and *zite*.

Noodles: Narrow, flat egg pasta strips of varying widths, straight or coiled into nests; some with attractive wavy edges. *Pappardelle* are the broadest noodles. *Tagliatelle* and *fettucine* are the most common types. Not all noodles are made from pasta flour; oriental noodles, for example, are often made from rice flour or mung beans.

Vermicelli: Very fine pasta strands, thinner than spaghetti, usually sold in nests; *capelli d'angelo* (angel's hair) is similar. *Paglia e fieno* (straw and hay) are nests of fine plain egg and green pasta.

Lasagne: Flat sheets of pasta, available in broad strips, rectangles and squares, straight or wavy edged. Usually made with egg pasta; *lasagne verde* (spinach pasta) is widely available too. Used in oven-baked dishes; some varieties do not require pre-cooking before baking. *Lasagnette* is a narrower version which is currently a popular alternative to tagliatelle.

Cannelloni are large hollow tubes of egg pasta which are typically filled with a stuffing and baked. *Rigatoni* are narrower tubes.

Stuffed pasta shapes: These include *ravioli* (squares) and *raviolini* (semi-circles), which may have plain or serrated edges. *Tortelloni* are made from stuffed rounds or squares, which are especially folded to give their characteristic shape.

Small pasta shapes: These are numerous and include *cappelletti* (little hats); *cavatappi* (short ridged twists); *conchiglie* (shells); *farfalle* (bows); *fusilli* (twists); *lumache* (snails); *orecchiette* (ears); *pipe* (curved tubes); *rotelle* (wheels) and *torchiette* (torches).

Pastina: Tiny pasta shapes used mainly in soups. These include *corallini* (rings); *orzo* or *puntalette* (rice grain shapes); and *stellette* (stars).

CHOICE OF SHAPES AND SIZES

The choice of pasta is largely a matter of personal taste, but you will find that some pasta shapes are more suited to particular recipes than others. Large shapes and wide noodles, for example, tend to work best in dishes where the other ingredients are chunky. Smoother-textured sauces are generally better served with finer pastas, such as spaghetti or linguine. Where a recipe includes a lot of sauce, shapes such as shells and tubes are ideal because they hold the sauce well.

QUANTITIES

It is difficult to give specific quantity guidelines for pasta, because there are so many factors, including the nature of the sauce and whether you are serving the pasta as a starter, lunch or main meal. Individual appetites for pasta seem to vary enormously too. As a very approximate guide, allow about 75-125 g (3-4 oz) uncooked weight per person.

COOKING PASTA

All pasta, fresh and dried, should be cooked until *al dente* – firm to the bite, definitely not soft, and without a hard, uncooked centre. Always add pasta to a large pan containing plenty of fast-boiling water; insufficient water will result in stodgy unevenly cooked pasta. Fresh pasta needs only the briefest of cooking, so watch it carefully. Most dried pasta takes around 8-12 minutes. Manufacturer's recommended cooking times provide a rough guide, but the only way to determine when pasta is cooked is by tasting. Avoid overcooking at all costs!

SERVING SUGGESTIONS

Have warmed serving plates or bowls ready as pasta quickly loses its heat once it is drained. Toss the pasta with the chosen sauce, butter or olive oil as soon as it is cooked, or it may start to stick together. If on the other hand you are cooking pasta to serve cold, drain and rinse with cold water to prevent further cooking and rinse off surface starch.

Parmesan cheese is almost an essential finishing touch to most pasta dishes. It may be expensive, but a little goes a long way, and a well-wrapped chunk of Parmesan will keep in the refrigerator for several weeks. Vegetarian Parmesan is available from healthfood shops. Either grate the Parmesan over the finished dish or shave off thin flakes, using a swivel potato peeler.

BASIC PASTA DOUGH

Pasta dough can either be made by hand, in a food processor with a dough attachment, or in a large mixer with a dough hook. Initially it is probably best to make the dough by hand to learn how the dough should feel at each stage. The more you make fresh pasta the easier it will be to judge the correct texture of the dough – it should be soft, not at all sticky, and with a good elasticity.

The best type of flour to use for making pasta is a very fine-textured soft wheat flour "type 00" or "*farino tipo 00*", available from Italian delicatessens and some larger supermarkets. Strong plain flour can be used as a substitute if necessary, although you may need to add a little more or a little less water.

This recipe makes 400 g (14 oz) pasta which is sufficient to serve 4 a main course, accompanied by a side salad and bread.

Serves 4
Preparation 5 minutes, plus kneading
Cooking 1-2 minutes
285 calories per serving

225 g (8 oz) type "00" pasta flour, plus extra for dusting
5 ml (1 tsp) salt
2 eggs, plus 1 egg yolk (size 3), beaten

15 ml (1 tbsp) extra-virgin olive oil
15-30 ml (1-2 tbsp) cold water

1 Sift the flour and salt into a bowl, make a well in the centre and add the eggs, egg yolk, oil and 15 ml (1 tbsp) water. Gradually work into the flour, adding a little extra water if necessary to form a soft but not sticky dough.
2 Transfer to a lightly floured surface and knead for about 5 minutes until the dough is firm smooth and elastic. Form into a flattish ball, wrap in cling film and leave to rest in the refrigerator for at least 30 minutes.

USING A FOOD PROCESSOR

Sift the flour and salt into the processor bowl and add the eggs, egg yolk, oil and 15 ml (1 tbsp) water (together with any flavourings). Process just until the dough begins to come together, adding the extra water if necessary to form a soft but not sticky dough. Wrap in cling film and rest (as above).

VARIATIONS

Making flavoured pastas is great fun and the choice is enormous. Fresh herbs such as basil, rosemary and dill are particularly good. Vegetable purées, such as beetroot and spinach, and flavoured pastes, like sun-dried tomato and olive, produce vibrant coloured pastas which have a delicious flavour. Note that some of the colour will be lost during cooking, without detriment to the flavour.

Fresh Herb Pasta

Sift the flour and salt into the bowl and stir in 45 ml (3 tbsp) freshly chopped mixed herbs, such as tarragon, marjoram and parsley. Continue as above.

Garlic and Basil Pasta

Sift the flour and salt into a bowl, stir in 15 g (½ oz) freshly chopped basil and 1 small crushed garlic clove. Continue as above.

Lemon Pasta

Sift the flour and salt into a bowl, then stir in the finely grated rind of 2 unwaxed lemons. Continue as above, replacing the water with 30 ml (2 tbsp) lemon juice.

Saffron Pasta

Sift the flour and salt into a bowl and stir in 5 ml (1 tsp) saffron strands. Continue as above.

Olive Pasta	Beat the eggs with 30 ml (2 tbsp) black olive paste before adding to the flour. Reduce the water to about 10 ml (2 tsp).
Sun-Dried Tomato Pasta	Beat the eggs with 30 ml (2 tbsp) sun-dried tomato paste before adding to the flour. Reduce the water to about 10 ml (2 tsp).
Black Peppercorn Pasta	Sift the flour and salt into a bowl. Roughly grind 10 ml (2 tsp) black peppercorns using a pestle and mortar or spice grinder. Stir into the flour and continue as above.
Buckwheat Pasta	Sift 150 g (5 oz) type "00" pasta flour and the salt into a bowl, then stir in 85 g (3 oz) buckwheat flour. Increase the amount of water to 30-45 ml (2-3 tbsp) and continue to work in the remaining ingredients, as above.
Beetroot Pasta	Purée 25 g (1 oz) cooked beetroot until very smooth and pass through a sieve, if necessary. Sift the flour and salt into a bowl, then gradually work in the beetroot paste with the rest of the ingredients, omitting the water. Continue as above.
Spinach Pasta	Blanch 50 g (2 oz) spinach leaves until wilted. Refresh under cold water, drain and squeeze out all excess water, then finely chop the spinach. Add to the flour and salt, together with the remaining ingredients. Continue as above.
Squid Ink Pasta	Add one sachet of squid ink to the beaten eggs before adding to the flour. Reduce the water to about 10 ml (2 tsp)

DRIED PASTA SHAPES
(key to pages 8-9)

1 Cannelloni
2 Rigatoni
3 Long Fusilli
4 Pastina
5 Conchiglioni
6 Tagliatelle
7 Pappardelle
8 Cappelletti
9 Corallini
10 Lasagnette
11 Torchiette
12 Bucatini
13 Spaghetti
14 Spaghettini
15 Fusilli

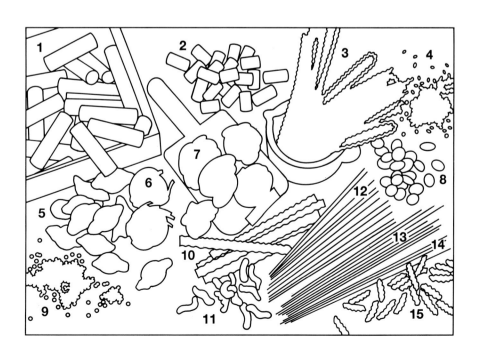

ROLLING OUT PASTA DOUGH USING A PASTA MACHINE

Most pasta machines work in the same way and this method should therefore apply, but do refer to the manufacturer's instructions for your particular model.

1 Divide the rested dough into 8 equal pieces; re-wrap all except one piece in cling film to prevent it from drying out.

2 Flatten the piece of dough slightly, so that it will fit through the pasta machine. With the rollers set at the widest setting, pass the pasta through. Fold the strip of dough in three, rotate and pass through the machine on this widest setting once more. The dough should now be smooth and of an even thickness.

3 Continue to pass the pasta through the machine in this way, narrowing the roller setting by one notch each time, and flouring the dough a little if it starts to feel sticky. Guide the dough through the machine with your hands, but do not pull it or the dough may drag and tear.

4 Pass the dough just once through the final narrowest setting to form a long thin sheet of pasta. For spaghetti and tagliatelle, the last but one setting is generally preferred. (If you are a beginner you may find it easier to stop at this setting anyway until you are happy to handle very thin dough.) For filled pastas, such as ravioli, the pasta should be rolled to the finest setting.

5 If making filled pasta, the dough should be used straight away, while it is a little sticky – to help the ravioli, etc adhere.

Otherwise, drape the sheet of pasta over a narrow wooden pole or pasta dryer and leave to dry slightly, for 3-5 minutes; this makes it easier to cut the pasta and prevents the strands from sticking together.
Alternatively, lay the pasta on a clean tea-towel for 5-10 minutes.

6 Repeat the process with the remaining dough to form 8 thin sheets.

ROLLING PASTA DOUGH BY HAND

1 Divide the dough into 4 equal pieces; re-wrap all except one piece in cling film to prevent it from drying out.

2 Roll out on a clean surface to a 5 mm (¼ inch) thickness. Lift the dough from the surface and rotate 45°. The dough should cling slightly (not stick) to the surface; this helps the stretching process.

3 Continue rolling, lifting and rotating the dough until it is a very thin square, approximately 30 x 30 cm (12 x 12 inches). The dough should be so thin that you could almost read print through it!

4 Repeat the process with the remaining dough to form 4 thin sheets. Leave to dry slightly if necessary (see above).

Shaping Ravioli

Cut one long thin sheet of pasta in half widthways. Lay one half on a well floured surface and position 5 spoonfuls of filling at 5 cm (2 inch) intervals, along the length of the pasta. Using a dampened pastry brush, moisten the pasta all around the filling.

Carefully position the second pasta sheet over the top of the filled sheet. Using your fingers, press firmly along the edges of the pasta and around the mounds of filling to seal the parcels.

Using a fluted pastry wheel or sharp knife, cut between the stuffing and neatly along the long edges. Alternatively, use a 7.5 cm (3 inch) plain or fluted ravioli cutter to stamp out around each parcel and form the ravioli. Repeat with the remaining dough and filling.

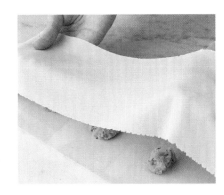

Shaping Raviolini

Using a fluted 7.5 cm (3 inch) round metal pastry cutter, stamp out circles of dough from the pasta sheet.

Spoon a small mound of stuffing onto the middle of each pasta round and moisten the edges of the pasta with a little water.

Fold each round in half to give a semi-circular shape, enclosing the filling. Press the edges together lightly to seal.

Shaping Noodles

If using a pasta machine, fit the tagliatelle or linguine cutters, as required. Take one sheet of dough and pass through the cutters. Hang the noodles over a pole and repeat with the remaining pasta sheets. Take the noodles a handful at a time and curl them directly onto a well floured tea-towel into a 'nest' shape. The noodles are now ready to cook.

To shape noodles by hand, flour the dough and roll up loosely as for a Swiss roll. Using a large sharp knife, cut into slices, the thickness depending on the noodles required. For linguine, cut into 5 mm (¼ inch) slices; for tagliatelle cut 8 mm (⅓ inch) slices; for the wider pappardelle noodles, cut 2 cm (¾ inch) slices. Alternatively, pappardelle can be cut directly from the flat square of pasta, using a pasta wheel.

Unroll the noodles and leave to hang over a wooden pole for up to 5 minutes to dry out. Curl into `nests' directly onto a well floured tea-towel.

Shaping Lasagne Sheets

Simply trim the pasta sheets to neaten and cut into lengths according to the size of your lasagne dish, using a sharp knife or a pasta wheel. Sheets measuring about 10 x 15 cm (4 x 6 inches) are easy to use.

Shaping Quills

Cut the pasta dough into 4 cm (1½ inch) squares. Lay the end of a wooden spoon handle diagonally across the square. Roll the pasta square around the handle to form a quill shape, pressing the corners together to seal. Repeat with the remaining squares. Allow to dry before cooking.

Shaping Tortelloni

Cut the pasta dough into 7.5 cm (3 inch) squares. Place a teaspoonful of filling in the middle of each square and moisten the edges of the dough with a little water. Fold each square diagonally in half over the filling to form a triangle. Press the edges together to seal. Curve the semi-circle around your finger and pinch the ends together, moistening them slightly; at the same time turn the sealed edge up to form a neat curved parcel.

PASTA AS AN ACCOMPANIMENT

Served as an accompaniment, pasta makes a welcome change from rice or potatoes. Piping hot noodles are delicious simply tossed with butter and coarsely ground black pepper, perhaps with a sprinkling of chopped fresh herbs. Alternatively, try one of the following original suggestions.

Pasta with Pine Nuts and Parmesan

Serves 4-6
Preparation 5 minutes
Cooking About 10 minutes
290-350 calories per serving

Serve this versatile accompaniment with grilled meats and vegetables, casseroles, meatballs and burgers.

350 g (12 oz) dried vermicelli or pasta noodles

salt and pepper

50 g (2 oz) pine nuts or flaked almonds, toasted

50 g (2 oz) Parmesan cheese, freshly grated or pared

1 Add the pasta to a large pan of boiling salted water and cook until *al dente*.
2 Drain well and toss with the pine nuts and Parmesan cheese.

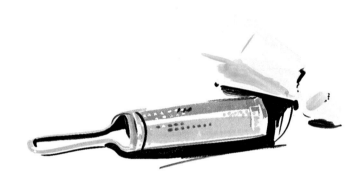

Pappardelle with Spinach

Serves 6
Preparation 5 minutes
Cooking About 10 minutes
350 calories per serving

Prepared in minutes, a generous bowlful of noodles with spinach is an excellent accompaniment to rich meat and vegetable stews, grilled fish and meat.

450 g (1 lb) dried pappardelle

salt and pepper

350 g (12 oz) spinach leaves, trimmed and roughly chopped

30 ml (2 tbsp) olive oil

1 Add the pappardelle to a large saucepan of boiling salted water and cook until *al dente*.
2 Drain the pasta and return to the pan. Add the spinach with just the water clinging to the leaves after washing, and the olive oil. Toss for 10-15 seconds or until just wilted. Adjust the seasoning and serve immediately.

Browned Noodles with Feta and Pepper

Serves 6
Preparation 10 minutes
Cooking 10 minutes
420 calories per serving

A quick and easy dish of tagliatelle fried in butter until browning, then tossed with crumbled feta cheese and ground mixed peppers. An ideal snack or accompaniment to grilled chicken, steak or veal.

400 g (14 oz) fresh or dried tagliatelle
salt
75 g (3 oz) butter

225 g (8 oz) feta cheese, cubed
5 ml (1 tsp) mixed peppercorns, ground

1 Cook the pasta in a large pan of boiling salted water until *al dente*. Drain well.
2 Meanwhile, melt the butter in a large pan and cook until just turning pale brown. Add the pasta and toss well to coat with the butter. Fry over a high heat for a few minutes until the pasta begins to brown.
3 Toss the browned noodles with the feta and ground peppercorns. Check for seasoning – as feta is quite salty, you may not need to add salt. Serve immediately.

Special Fried Noodles

Serves 6
Preparation 10 minutes
Cooking About 10 minutes
225 calories per serving

Serve as an accompaniment to Chinese dishes, plain grilled fish and chicken.

150 g (5 oz) medium egg noodles
30 ml (2 tbsp) oil
1 large red chilli, seeded and chopped
175 g (6 oz) shallots or onions, peeled and finely chopped
4 garlic cloves, peeled and crushed
125 g (4 oz) cabbage, finely shredded
125 g (4 oz) carrots, peeled and finely sliced

225 g (8 oz) cooked peeled prawns (optional)
125 g (4 oz) bean sprouts
salt and pepper
DRESSING
15 ml (1 tbsp) caster sugar
15 ml (1 tbsp) tomato ketchup
15 ml (1 tbsp) soy sauce

1 Cook the noodles according to the packet instructions; rinse and drain.
2 To make the dressing, mix together the sugar, tomato ketchup and soy sauce in a bowl.
3 Heat the oil in a large frying pan over a high heat. Add the chilli, shallots and garlic, and cook, stirring, for 2 minutes or until golden.
4 Stir in the cabbage and carrots and cook, stirring, for about 4 minutes. Stir in the noodles, prawns and bean sprouts, together with the dressing. Toss over a high heat for 1-2 minutes to heat through.
5 Adjust the seasoning and serve immediately.

CLASSIC PASTA SAUCES

These simple, classic sauces form the basis of some of the pasta recipes in the following chapters. Tossed with your favourite pasta – plain or flavoured – they also make tasty lunch or supper dishes in their own right.

Fresh Tomato Sauce

Serves 4
Preparation 10 minutes
Cooking About 1 hour
105 calories per serving

During the summer months when tomatoes are plentiful and at their best, make up several quantities of this sauce and freeze for use during the winter.

900 g (2 lb) vine-ripened tomatoes, roughly chopped
30 ml (2 tbsp) extra-virgin olive oil
2 garlic cloves, peeled and crushed
grated rind of 1 lemon

5 ml (1 tsp) dried oregano
30 ml (2 tbsp) chopped fresh basil
salt and pepper
pinch of sugar, or to taste (optional)

1 Put the tomatoes, olive oil, garlic, lemon rind and oregano in a saucepan. Bring to the boil, cover and simmer gently for 30 minutes.
2 Add the basil, salt and pepper to taste and a little sugar if required. Simmer, uncovered, for a further 20-30 minutes until the sauce is thickened. If a smooth sauce is preferred, pass through a sieve.
3 Toss the sauce with freshly cooked pasta to serve. Accompany with freshly grated Parmesan cheese.

Rich Tomato Sauce

Serves 4-6
Preparation 10-15 minutes
Cooking 25-30 minutes
175-115 calories per serving

Made with fresh tomato and enriched with sun-dried tomato paste, this sauce is substantial enough to serve on plain pasta as a meal, but it is also good served with filled pastas such as ravioli, tortelloni, cannelloni etc. Full-flavoured ripe, fresh tomatoes give the best result but canned plum tomatoes are a better choice than under-ripe or flavourless fresh ones. The sauce is suitable for freezing.

50 g (2 oz) butter
1 onion, peeled and finely chopped
2 garlic cloves, peeled and finely chopped
1 kg (2 lb) ripe tomatoes, preferably plum, or two 397 (14 oz) cans plum tomatoes with their juice

45 ml (3 tbsp) sun-dried tomato paste (see note)
2 oregano sprigs
salt and pepper

1 Melt the butter in a saucepan, add the onion and garlic and cook over a medium-low heat for about 8 minutes while preparing the tomatoes.
2 If using fresh tomatoes, first skin them. Immerse in a bowl of boiling water for 30 seconds, then drain and refresh under cold running water. Peel away the skins. Quarter the tomatoes, discard the seeds, then roughly chop the flesh. If using canned plum tomatoes, chop them roughly.
3 Add the tomatoes to the onion and garlic mixture together with the sun-dried tomato paste and oregano sprigs. Cook, uncovered, over a low heat for 25-30 minutes, stirring occasionally, until the sauce is thick and pulpy. Discard the oregano and season with salt and pepper to taste.
4 Toss with hot pasta and serve topped with shavings of Parmesan and chopped parsley.

NOTE: Jars of sun-dried tomato paste are available from larger supermarkets and Italian delicatessens, but it's also very easy to make your own. Simply purée the contents of a jar of sun-dried tomatoes in oil, using a food processor or blender. You may prefer to drain off some of the oil first to get a good thick paste, but don't throw it away as it has a great flavour. Return the paste to the empty jar and store in the refrigerator until required.

Quick Tomato Sauce

Serves 4
Preparation 10-15 minutes
Cooking 35 minutes
100 calories per serving

15 ml (1 tbsp) olive oil
75 g (3 oz) onion, peeled and chopped
75 g (3 oz) celery, chopped
75 g (3 oz) carrot, peeled and chopped
1 garlic clove, peeled and crushed

two 400 g (14 oz) cans chopped tomatoes
30 ml (2 tbsp) tomato purée
150 ml (¼ pint) vegetable stock
100 ml (3½ fl oz) dry red wine
salt and pepper

1 Heat the olive oil in a large saucepan. Add the vegetables and garlic and cook, stirring occasionally, for 5 minutes or until beginning to soften, but not coloured.

2 Stir in the canned tomatoes, tomato purée, stock, wine and seasoning to taste. Simmer, covered, for about 30 minutes, stirring occasionally.

3 If a smooth-textured sauce is required, transfer to a blender or food processor and work until smooth.

4 Return the sauce to the pan and heat through. Check the seasoning before tossing with freshly cooked pasta. Serve topped with freshly grated Parmesan.

VARIATIONS
Add 1 small, finely diced red chilli with the garlic at stage 1.
Add 125 g (4 oz) sautéed sliced mushrooms and 30 ml (2 tbsp) chopped parsley at the beginning of stage 4.

Classic Beef Ragu

Serves 4-6
Preparation 20 minutes, plus soaking
Cooking About 1 hour
655-435 calories per serving

This traditional meat sauce may take a little longer to prepare than the simplified version opposite, but it has a superb flavour and is well worth the effort. For convenience, it may be prepared ahead and frozen; defrost thoroughly at room temperature before reheating.

10 g (⅓ oz) dried porcini mushrooms
15 ml (1 tbsp) olive oil
275 g (10 oz) onion, peeled and finely chopped
75 g (3 oz) carrot, peeled and finely chopped
75 g (3 oz) celery, finely chopped
125 g (4 oz) brown-cap or large button mushrooms, chopped
2 garlic cloves, peeled and crushed
125 g (4 oz) rindless streaky bacon, chopped

450 g (1 lb) minced beef
300 ml (½ pint) dry white wine
300 ml (½ pint) stock
15 ml (1 tbsp) tomato purée
10 ml (2 tsp) dried oregano
125 g (4 oz) chicken livers, trimmed and chopped
90 ml (6 tbsp) double cream
30 ml (2 tbsp) chopped fresh parsley
salt and pepper

1 Put the dried porcini mushrooms in a bowl, pour on 100 ml (3 ½ fl oz) water and leave to soak for about 30 minutes.

2 Heat the oil in a frying pan. Add the onion, carrot and celery and fry gently for 5 minutes, or until softened. Add the fresh mushrooms and garlic; fry for 1 minute.

3 Add the bacon and beef; cook, stirring, over a high heat until browned. Stir in the wine, stock, tomato purée and oregano. Bring to the boil, cover and simmer for 45 minutes.

4 Stir in the dried mushrooms with their liquor, and the chicken livers. Simmer, uncovered, for 7-10 minutes, until the livers are cooked and the liquid is reduced by half. Add the cream and parsley and allow to bubble for 1 minute.

5 Check the seasoning, before serving with spaghetti, tagliatelle or other pasta. Accompany with freshly grated Parmesan.

Simple Bolognese Sauce

Serves 4
Preparation 10 minutes
Cooking About 1 hour
340 calories per serving

For instant suppers, keep a stock of this sauce in the freezer. It can be defrosted quickly in the microwave.

15 ml (1 tbsp) olive oil
1 large onion, peeled and finely chopped
1 carrot, peeled and finely chopped
1 celery stick, finely chopped
1 garlic clove, peeled and crushed
125 g (4 oz) button mushrooms, chopped
450 g (1 lb) minced beef
300 ml (½ pint) beef stock

300 ml (½ pint) dry red or white wine
400 g (14 oz) can chopped tomatoes
15 ml (1 tbsp) tomato purée
10 ml (2 tsp) dried oregano
salt and pepper
30 ml (2 tbsp) chopped fresh parsley

1 Heat the oil in a frying pan. Add the onion, carrot, celery and garlic, and fry gently for 5 minutes, or until softened. Add the mushrooms and fry for 1 minute.
2 Stir in the beef and cook, stirring, over a high heat until browned. Stir in the stock, wine, tomatoes, tomato purée, oregano and seasoning. Bring to the boil, cover and simmer for 1 hour or until the meat is tender and the sauce is well reduced.
3 Check the seasoning and stir in the parsley before serving with spaghetti, tagliatelle or other pasta. Accompany with freshly grated Parmesan.

Pesto

Serves 4
Preparation 10-15 minutes
380 calories per serving

A classic sauce to serve with plain or filled pasta as a starter, supper dish or quick lunch. Jars (and tubs) of ready-made pesto are available, but nothing can compare with the flavour of freshly made pesto.

50 g (2 oz) fresh basil leaves, roughly chopped
2 garlic cloves, peeled
30 ml (2 tbsp) pine nuts, toasted
120 ml (4 fl oz) extra-virgin olive oil

salt and pepper
50 g (2 oz) Parmesan cheese, freshly grated
squeeze of lemon juice (optional)

1 Put the basil, garlic and pine nuts in a mortar with a little of the oil and pound with a pestle to a paste. Alternatively, work in a food processor to a fairly smooth paste.
2 Work in the rest of the oil and season with salt and pepper to taste.
3 Transfer to a bowl and fold in the cheese. Check the seasoning and add a squeeze of lemon juice if desired.
4 Store for up to 2 weeks in the refrigerator in a screw-topped jar, covered with a thin layer of oil.

VARIATION
CHILLI PESTO: Add 2 seeded and chopped chillies at stage 1. Omit the Parmesan cheese.

Rocket Pesto

Serves 4
Preparation 10-15 minutes
215 calories per serving

50 g (2 oz) rocket, roughly chopped
1 garlic clove, peeled
15 ml (1 tbsp) capers, rinsed and drained
15 ml (1 tbsp) chopped fresh parsley

15 g (½ oz) pine nuts, toasted
15 g (½ oz) pecorino or Parmesan cheese, freshly grated
75 ml (5 tbsp) extra-virgin olive oil
salt and pepper

1 Put the rocket in a mortar, grinder or food processor with the garlic, capers, parsley, pine nuts and cheese. Work to a fairly smooth paste, then stir in the oil and season with salt and pepper to taste.

QUICK AND SIMPLE PASTA

Spaghetti alla Carbonara

Serves 4-6
Preparation 10 minutes
Cooking 10 minutes
675-450 calories per serving

Illustrated on page 21

This classic Italian pasta dish – with its rich smoky flavour and light, soft scrambled egg texture – is cooked as it should be, with the residual heat of the spaghetti setting the eggs to give a creamy sauce. If pecorino cheese is unobtainable, simply double the quantity of Parmesan.

30 ml (2 tbsp) extra-virgin olive oil
25 g (1 oz) butter
125-150 g (4-5 oz) smoked pancetta (see note), derinded and cut into strips
1 garlic clove, peeled and halved
3 eggs
30 ml (2 tbsp) dry white wine

30 ml (2 tbsp) chopped fresh parsley
40 g (1½ oz) Parmesan cheese, grated
40 g (1½ oz) pecorino cheese, grated
salt and pepper
400 g (14 oz) dried spaghetti

1 Heat the oil and butter in a heavy-based pan. Add the pancetta and garlic and cook over a medium heat for 3-4 minutes until the pancetta begins to crisp. Turn off the heat; discard the garlic.
2 Meanwhile, in a bowl, beat the eggs with the wine, parsley and half of each of the cheeses. Season with salt and pepper.
3 Cook the spaghetti in a large pan of boiling salted water until *al dente*.
4 When the spaghetti is almost cooked, gently reheat the pancetta in the pan. Drain the spaghetti thoroughly, then return to the pan. Immediately add the egg mixture with the pancetta. Off the heat, toss well until the eggs are creamy. Add the remaining cheeses, toss lightly and serve at once.

NOTE: Smoked pancetta is obtainable from Italian delicatessens. If it is not available use smoked bacon but you will need to increase the quantity to 175 - 225 g (6 - 8 oz) to give sufficient flavour.

Spaghetti with Garlic

Serves 6
Preparation 5 minutes
Cooking 10 minutes
370 calories per serving

Increase or decrease the quantity of garlic and chilli used in this intensely flavoured dish according to taste. Serve with a crisp mixed leaf salad as a fast lunch or supper dish.

450 g (1 lb) dried spaghetti
salt and pepper
75 ml (5 tbsp) virgin olive oil
2 garlic cloves, peeled and crushed

1 fresh chilli, seeded and chopped
30 ml (2 tbsp) chopped fresh parsley, coriander or basil (optional)

1 Cook the spaghetti in a large pan of boiling salted water for 8-10 minutes or until *al dente*.
2 Meanwhile, heat the oil in a heavy-based saucepan. Add the garlic and chilli, and fry for 3-4 minutes, stirring occasionally; do not allow the garlic or chilli to become too brown or the oil will taste bitter. Remove from the heat and set aside until the pasta is cooked.
3 Drain the pasta thoroughly. Reheat the oil over a very high heat for 1 minute, then pour over the pasta with the herbs, if using. Season with salt and pepper and serve immediately.

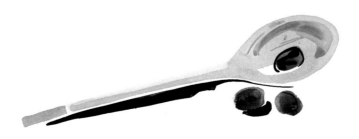

Spaghetti with Fresh Tomato and Olive Sauce

Serves 4
Preparation 10 minutes, plus standing
Cooking 10 minutes
725 calories per serving

Although this sauce is not cooked, the heat from the pasta will release the delicious flavours.

4 large ripe tomatoes
125 g (4 oz) pitted black Greek-style olives, roughly chopped
2 garlic cloves, peeled and finely chopped
60 ml (4 tbsp) chopped fresh basil
150 ml (¼ pint) olive oil
salt and pepper
400 g (14 oz) spaghetti

1 Immerse the tomatoes in boiling water for 30 seconds-1 minute (no longer or they will go too mushy). Lift out with a slotted spoon and plunge into a bowl of cold water. Peel off the skins and dry the tomatoes on kitchen paper.
2 Halve the tomatoes and squeeze out the seeds, then chop into 5 mm (¼ inch) cubes.
3 Mix the tomatoes, olives, garlic, basil, olive oil and seasoning together in a non-metallic bowl. Cover and leave for at least 30 minutes to allow the flavours time to mellow.
4 Cook the pasta in a large pan of boiling salted water until *al dente*. Drain and toss with the sauce. Cover with a lid and leave to stand for 2-3 minutes. Toss again and serve immediately.

Note: It is essential to use really red ripe flavourful tomatoes – avoid small hard tomatoes that have little flavour at all cost!

Fusilli with Asparagus and Parmesan

Serves 4-6
Preparation 5 minutes
Cooking 10 minutes
875-585 calories per serving

Asparagus is a wonderful vegetable – its presence in a dish always adds a touch of extravagance – even to a simple pasta dish like this! Long, curly fusilli is a pretty pasta shape to use – and retains its firmness when cooked and tossed in a sauce. Serve this dish as a lunch or quick supper with a crisp leafy salad.

400 g (14 oz) pencil-thin asparagus, trimmed
salt and pepper
50 g (2 oz) butter
1 onion, peeled and finely chopped
90 ml (3 fl oz) dry white wine
400 g (14 oz) dried long fusilli, tagliatelle or penne
300 ml (½ pint) extra-thick double cream
50 g (2 oz) Parmesan cheese, freshly grated

1 Heat a 2 cm (¾ inch) depth of water in a frying pan. Add a pinch of salt and bring to the boil. Add the asparagus spears and cook for 4-5 minutes until almost tender. Drain, reserving 75 ml (5 tbsp) of the cooking water. Cut the asparagus into 5 cm (2 inch) lengths and set aside.
2 Melt the butter in the frying pan. Add the onion and cook over a medium high heat for about 5 minutes until softened and beginning to colour. Stir in the asparagus and cook for 1 minute. Pour in the reserved cooking water and the wine. Cook over a high heat until almost all the liquid has evaporated.
3 Meanwhile, cook the pasta in a large pan of boiling salted water until *al dente*.
4 Add the cream to the sauce, stir well and heat until bubbling. Stir in half of the grated Parmesan and salt and pepper to taste.
5 Drain the pasta thoroughly and add to the sauce. Toss well to mix. Serve at once, sprinkled with the remaining Parmesan and pepper to taste.

VARIATION
Add 75 g (3 oz) derinded and diced smoked pancetta or thick-cut smoked streaky bacon at stage 2, with the onion.

Orecchiette with Rocket and Cherry Tomatoes

Serves 4
Preparation 10 minutes
Cooking About 10 minutes
580 calories per serving

Illustrated opposite

This quick, fresh-tasting dish relies on the inclusion of peppery rocket leaves or *roquette* for its success. Available in many supermarkets, rocket is also easy to grow in the garden or in a window box. Serve this pasta dish as a light lunch, accompanied by a crisp leafy salad and warm crusty bread.

400 g (14 oz) dried orecchiette
salt and pepper
45 ml (3 tbsp) olive oil
30 ml (2 tbsp) pine nuts

450 g (1 lb) very ripe cherry tomatoes, halved
75 g (3 oz) rocket leaves
50 g (2 oz) Parmesan cheese, freshly pared, to serve

1 Cook the pasta in a large pan of boiling salted water until *al dente*.
2 A few minutes before the pasta will be ready, heat 30 ml (2 tbsp) of the oil in a large saucepan. Add the pine nuts and cook for 1-2 minutes until golden. Add the tomatoes and cook for barely 1 minute until only just heated through, not disintegrated.
3 Drain the pasta thoroughly and toss with the remaining olive oil. Add the pasta to the tomatoes, then add the rocket. Carefully stir to mix and heat through. Season generously with salt and pepper. Serve immediately, topped with plenty of Parmesan shavings.

VARIATION
Use young spinach leaves in place of the rocket.

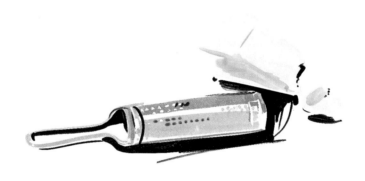

Tomato Pasta with Summer Vegetables

Serves 4
Preparation 5 minutes
Cooking 10 minutes
470 calories per serving

Freshly picked mint from the garden adds a summery freshness to this delicious mid-week supper dish.

350 g (12 oz) dried pasta, such as rigatoni or penne
salt and pepper
30 ml (2 tbsp) olive oil
175 g (6 oz) sugar snap peas or mangetouts
250 g (9 oz) cherry tomatoes, halved

60 ml (4 tbsp) sun-dried tomato paste

TO SERVE
30 ml (1-2 tbsp) chopped fresh mint
freshly grated Parmesan cheese

1 Cook the pasta in a large pan of boiling salted water until *al dente*.
2 Meanwhile, heat the olive oil in a frying pan, add the sugar snap peas or mangetouts and cook, stirring, for 1-2 minutes. Add the cherry tomatoes and sun-dried tomato paste and cook for 1 minute.
3 Drain the pasta thoroughly. Toss with the vegetables and chopped mint and season liberally with salt and pepper. Serve sprinkled with freshly grated Parmesan cheese.

Pasta with Courgettes and Balsamic Vinegar

Serves 4-6
Preparation 10 minutes
Cooking 25 minutes
725-480 calories per serving

Courgettes are cooked until meltingly soft and their sweet flavour is enlivened with the addition of balsamic vinegar. Small to medium courgettes work best in this dish and, for the pasta, choose either large ribbons, such as tagliatelle or pappardelle, or shapes such as tubes or twists.

75 ml (5 tbsp) extra-virgin olive oil
45 ml (3 tbsp) pine nuts
1 small onion, peeled and finely chopped
2 garlic cloves, peeled and finely chopped
450 g (1 lb) courgettes, thinly sliced
salt and pepper

45 ml (3 tbsp) chopped fresh parsley
400 g (14 oz) tagliatelle, pappardelle or pasta shapes
15-30 ml (1-2 tbsp) balsamic vinegar
90 ml (6 tbsp) freshly grated Parmesan or pecorino cheese

1 Heat 30 ml (2 tbsp) olive oil in a large frying pan. Add the pine nuts and cook, stirring, over a medium high heat for 2-3 minutes until lightly browned. Transfer to a small bowl and set aside.

2 Add the remaining oil to the pan. Stir in the onion and garlic and cook over a gentle heat for 2 minutes to soften. Add the courgettes and increase the heat. Cook, stirring, for about 4 minutes until just beginning to brown.

3 Add the seasoning, parsley and 30 ml (2 tbsp) water to the pan. Cover, lower the heat and cook gently for 15 minutes, stirring twice.

4 Meanwhile, cook the pasta in a large pan of boiling salted water until *al dente*. (Fresh pasta ribbons will need only 2-3 minutes cooking time.)

5 Uncover the courgettes and cook for a moment or two over a high heat, stirring gently, until excess liquid has evaporated. Remove from the heat and sprinkle with the balsamic vinegar and pine nuts.

6 Drain the pasta thoroughly and add to the courgettes with two thirds of the cheese. Toss to mix. Serve at once, sprinkled with the remaining cheese.

NOTE: Balsamic vinegar can be bought at reasonable prices in many supermarkets. If you are buying it from a specialist shop you may find prices vary, depending on the maturity of the vinegar. The longer the vinegar has been matured the more concentrated the flavour, so – although more expensive – you won't need to use as much.

Tomato Pappardelle with Olives

Serves 4-6
Preparation 10 minutes, plus pasta
Cooking 2-10 minutes
815-540 calories per serving

This simple, robust sauce of chopped olives, sun-dried tomatoes, capers, anchovies, chilli and parsley is superb with pasta. If you have sufficient time, make your own pappardelle. Serve as a starter or light meal.

150 g (5 oz) kalamata olives, pitted and chopped
8 sun-dried tomatoes in oil, drained and cut into thin strips
60 ml (4 tbsp) capers, chopped
4 anchovy fillets, chopped
1 mild red chilli, seeded and finely chopped
120 ml (8 tbsp) roughly chopped fresh parsley

150 ml (¼ pint) extra-virgin olive oil
salt and pepper
1 quantity fresh sun-dried tomato pappardelle (see page 11), or 400 g (14 oz) fresh or dried pappardelle
flat-leaf parsley, to garnish
crumbled pecorino cheese, to serve

1 Mix together the olives, sun-dried tomatoes, capers, anchovies, chilli, parsley, oil and seasoning.

2 Cook the pasta in a large saucepan of boiling salted water until *al dente*; fresh pasta will only take 1-2 minutes.

3 Drain the pasta and toss with the olive mixture. Serve garnished with the parsley and topped with the crumbled cheese.

Tagliatelle with Sage, Pimento and Garlic

Serves 4-6
Preparation 10 minutes
Cooking About 10 minutes
775-520 calories per serving

Canned pimentos lend a mellow flavour to this dish and provide a really fast alternative to grilled and skinned peppers. If you have the time and want to use fresh peppers instead, you'll need to grill and skin three large red ones.

60 ml (4 tbsp) extra-virgin olive oil
1 small onion, peeled and finely chopped
2 garlic cloves, peeled and finely chopped
400 g (14 oz) can pimentos in brine, drained, rinsed and diced
30 ml (2 tbsp) chopped fresh sage
150 ml (¼ pint) extra-thick double cream
75 ml (5 tbsp) freshly grated Parmesan cheese
salt and pepper
400 g (14 oz) green and plain tagliatelle
sage sprigs, to garnish

1 Heat the oil in a large frying pan. Add the onion and garlic and cook over a medium heat for about 5 minutes until softened; do not allow to brown.
2 Add the diced pimentos and chopped sage and continue cooking for 3 minutes. Stir in the cream and bring to a simmer, then stir in all but 15 ml (1 tbsp) of the grated Parmesan. Season with salt and pepper to taste.
3 Meanwhile, cook the pasta in a large pan of boiling salted water until *al dente*. (Fresh pasta will require only 1-2 minutes cooking time.)
4 To serve, drain the pasta thoroughly and add to the sauce. Toss well to mix. Serve sprinkled with the remaining Parmesan and garnished with sage leaves.

NOTE: Extra-thick double cream is used here and in other creamy sauces as it lends the correct consistency. If you prefer to use ordinary double cream, increase the quantity by about one third and reduce the creamy sauce slightly by simmering until the desired consistency is obtained.

VARIATION
Use pasta tubes, such as rigatoni or penne, in place of the tagliatelle and add 175 g (6 oz) diced mozzarella cheese to the sauce at the end of cooking. The cheese cubes should melt softly when tossed with the hot pasta but not disappear completely into the sauce.

Pasta with Courgettes in a Creamy Tomato Sauce

Serves 4-6
Preparation 20 minutes
Cooking About 15 minutes
895-595 calories per serving

Illustrated opposite

For this simple, delicately flavoured dish the vegetables must be sautéed gently until rich and buttery, with just a hint of colour. Vary the herbs as you like.

40 g (1½ oz) butter
1 small onion, peeled and finely chopped
2 garlic cloves, peeled and finely chopped
450 g (1 lb) courgettes, diced
400 g (14 oz) dried penne or other pasta
salt and pepper

4 tomatoes, skinned, seeded and chopped
45 ml (3 tbsp) chopped fresh parsley
30 ml (2 tbsp) chopped fresh dill
300 ml (½ pint) extra-thick double cream
90 ml (6 tbsp) freshly grated Parmesan or pecorino cheese

1 Heat the butter in a large sauté pan. Add the onion and garlic and cook over a gentle heat for 3 minutes until softened.
2 Add the courgettes, increase the heat and cook, stirring, for about 4 minutes until just beginning to brown, then lower the heat. Cover and cook for a further 3-4 minutes until the courgettes are very tender.
3 Meanwhile, cook the pasta in a large pan of boiling salted water until *al dente*.
4 Add the tomatoes and parsley to the courgette mixture and season with salt and pepper to taste. Lower the heat, cover and cook gently for 2 minutes, then stir in the dill and cream. Allow to bubble for 1 minute, then stir in two thirds of the cheese. Cook for 1 minute or so, until thickened.
5 Drain the cooked pasta thoroughly, add to the sauce and toss to mix. Serve at once, sprinkled with the remaining cheese.

VARIATIONS
Flavour the tomato sauce with different herbs, such as parsley and tarragon, or chervil and dill.

Fusilli with Mushrooms

Serves 4
Preparation 10 minutes
Cooking 15 minutes
500 calories per serving

Serve this effortless supper dish with a glass of robust Italian red wine and a crisp green salad.

30 ml (2 tbsp) olive oil
225 g (8 oz) brown cap mushrooms, roughly chopped
2 garlic cloves, peeled and crushed
45 ml (3 tbsp) black olive paste
10 ml (2 tsp) chilli paste

60 ml (4 tbsp) chopped fresh parsley
60 ml (4 tbsp) mascarpone cheese
salt and pepper
400 g (14 oz) dried fusilli or other pasta

1 Heat the oil in a frying pan, add the mushrooms and garlic, and cook for 3-4 minutes or until most of the liquid has evaporated. Remove from the heat and stir in the olive paste, chilli paste, parsley and mascarpone. Season with salt and pepper to taste, bearing in mind that the olive paste is quite salty.
2 Cook the pasta in a large pan of boiling salted water until *al dente*. Drain well and return to the pan.
3 Reheat the sauce briefly, if necessary, then add to the pasta and toss well to mix. Serve at once.

Pasta Dumplings with Garlic, Parsley and Chilli Sauce

Serves 4
Preparation 15 minutes
Cooking About 20 minutes
445 calories per serving

This recipe is based on a German dish called *spatzle*. To shape the dumplings, the dough is traditionally twisted between the fingers straight into the boiling water; here we improvise with a sharp knife. Plenty of garlic in the sauce makes this a real favourite!

DUMPLINGS
225 g (8 oz) plain flour
2.5 ml (½ tsp) salt
1 egg, beaten
60-90 ml (2-3 fl oz) water

SAUCE
90 ml (6 tbsp) extra-virgin olive oil
2 large garlic cloves, peeled and finely chopped
2 small red chillies, seeded and finely chopped
4 anchovy fillets, drained and finely chopped
60 ml (4 tbsp) chopped fresh parsley
salt and pepper

TO SERVE
freshly grated Parmesan cheese

1 Sift the flour and salt into a bowl and make a well in the centre. Add the egg and water and gradually work into the flour to form a soft dough; do not overwork or the dough will become tough. Cover with cling film and set aside.
2 Bring a large pan of water to the boil with 10 ml (2 tsp) salt added.
3 Meanwhile, heat the oil in a large frying pan, add the garlic, chillies and anchovies and sauté for 5 minutes; keep warm.
4 Divide the dough in half and roll out each piece on a floured surface to a 5 mm (¼ inch) thickness. Cut into thin strips with a sharp knife.
5 Cook the dumplings in batches: drop into the boiling water, return to the boil and cook for 5 minutes until they rise to the surface. Remove with a slotted spoon and add to the sauce. Repeat with the remaining dough.
6 Add the parsley. Heat through briefly and serve at once, with pepper and plenty of Parmesan.

VARIATION
Rather than make dumplings, toss the sauce with freshly cooked pasta.

Fried Paglia e Fieno with Rich Tomato Sauce

Serves 4
Preparation 10 minutes
Cooking 30-35 minutes
670 calories per serving

For this interesting alternative to Spaghetti Napoletana, pasta is shallow-fried until golden brown, then tossed in a rich tomato sauce. Try serving it with a bowl of Greek-style yogurt flavoured with garlic.

250 g (9 oz) fresh paglia e fieno, or any very fine fresh pasta
125-175 ml (4-6 fl oz) olive oil

SAUCE
45 ml (3 tbsp) olive oil
2 large onions, peeled and finely chopped
3 large garlic cloves, peeled and crushed
two 400 g (14 oz) cans peeled tomatoes, mashed (see note)
400 g (14 oz) can chopped tomatoes
45 ml (3 tbsp) tomato purée or sun-dried tomato paste
4 fresh oregano sprigs
4 fresh thyme sprigs
30-45 ml (2-3 tbsp) chopped fresh basil leaves
2 bay leaves
sugar, to taste
salt and pepper

1 To make the sauce, heat the oil in a large saucepan, add the onions and fry over a moderate heat for about 10 minutes until soft and transparent. Add the garlic and cook for 1 minute. Add the remaining ingredients and season lightly. Cover and simmer gently for 20-25 minutes, stirring occasionally. The sauce should be thick, but loose enough to drop off a wooden spoon easily. Discard the herb sprigs and bay leaves. Check the seasoning, adding a little sugar if necessary.
2 About halfway through simmering the sauce, cook the pasta in batches: pull apart and separate the pasta strands. Heat about 60 ml (4 tbsp) oil in a large heavy-based sauté pan until just beginning to smoke. Add a third of the pasta

(or as much as the pan will hold comfortably). Using two long-handled forks, pull, tease and turn the pasta over continuously until it is crisp and evenly pale golden brown in colour. Transfer to an ovenproof dish without draining; keep warm in a low oven. Repeat with the remaining pasta, heating another 60 ml (4 tbsp) oil in the pan each time.

3 Spoon the tomato sauce evenly over the pasta and toss minimally as the pasta will be brittle and break easily. Serve immediately.

NOTE: Canned cherry tomatoes, which are now available from some super-markets, would be ideal for this sauce, which is suitable for freezing.

Pappardelle with Artichokes, Parmesan and Cream

Serves 4-6
Preparation 5 minutes
Cooking 10 minutes
835-555 calories per serving

Served with a mixed leaf or tomato and basil salad and some rustic bread, this simple dish makes a quick and sustaining meal. If preferred, combine the sauce with a finer pasta, such as spaghetti or paglia e fieno.

400 g (14 oz) dried pappardelle or tagliatelle
salt and pepper
25 g (1 oz) butter
2 garlic cloves, peeled and finely chopped
12 artichoke hearts preserved in oil, drained and thinly sliced

45 ml (3 tbsp) chopped fresh parsley
300 ml (½ pint) extra-thick double cream
90 ml (6 tbsp) freshly grated pecorino or Parmesan cheese

1 Cook the pasta in a large pan of boiling salted water until *al dente*.
2 Meanwhile, prepare the sauce. Melt the butter in a large frying pan, add the chopped garlic and cook over a gentle heat for about 3 minutes to soften; do not allow to brown.
3 Add the artichokes and 30 ml (2 tbsp) of the chopped parsley to the frying pan. Cook, stirring, for 2 minutes. Stir in the cream and bring to a simmer. Stir in the grated cheese and cook for a further 1 minute. Season with salt and pepper to taste.
4 To serve, drain the pasta thoroughly. Add to the sauce and toss well to mix. Serve at once, sprinkled with the remaining chopped parsley.

NOTE: Artichoke hearts preserved in oil are available in jars from many supermarkets and are often sold 'loose' at Italian specialist shops. They are superior in flavour to canned artichoke hearts in brine which should not be used for this recipe.

VARIATION
Add 50-75 g (2-3 oz) roughly chopped walnuts to the sauce at stage 3, with the cheese. If available, use 45 ml (3 tbsp) walnut oil in place of the butter.

Pasta with Prawns, Garlic and Spinach

Serves 4
Preparation 5 minutes
Cooking 10 minutes
610 calories per serving

Illustrated opposite

To save time, buy a bag of ready-prepared spinach leaves for this delicious fast supper.

350 g (12 oz) spaghetti
salt and pepper
125 g (4 oz) butter
2 garlic cloves, peeled and crushed
225 g (8 oz) cooked peeled prawns

225 g (8 oz) spinach leaves, trimmed and chopped
30-45 ml (2-3 tbsp) chopped fresh parsley

1 Cook the spaghetti in a large pan of boiling salted water until *al dente*.
2 In a large saucepan, melt the butter with the garlic; then add the prawns and turn to coat with the butter. Heat through gently for 1 minute only.
3 Drain the spaghetti thoroughly and return to the pan. Add the spinach, buttered prawns and parsley. Season liberally with salt and pepper and toss well over the heat until the spinach wilts. Serve immediately.

Spaghetti with Smoked Salmon and Scrambled Eggs

Serves 4-6
Preparation 5 minutes
Cooking 10 minutes
540-360 calories per serving

In this classic dish, the eggs are softly scrambled in the residual heat of the pasta. Look out for inexpensive packets of smoked salmon trimmings which are ideal for this recipe.

400 g (14 oz) dried spaghetti
salt and pepper
3 eggs
30 ml (2 tbsp) chopped fresh parsley or dill

40 g (1½ oz) butter
125 g (4 oz) smoked salmon, cut into strips
freshly grated Parmesan cheese, to serve (optional)

1 Cook the spaghetti in a large pan of boiling salted water until *al dente*.
2 Meanwhile, in a bowl, beat the eggs with the parsley or dill.
3 When the spaghetti is cooked, drain thoroughly, then return to the pan and toss with the butter. Immediately add the beaten egg mixture and toss well, off the heat, until the eggs are creamy. Stir in the smoked salmon strips and freshly ground pepper to taste.
4 Serve at once, with freshly grated Parmesan if preferred.

Seafood Spaghetti with Pepper, Almond and Garlic Sauce

Serves 4-6
Preparation 20 minutes
Cooking 20 minutes
555-370 calories per serving

For speed and convenience, buy a bag of ready-prepared mixed cooked seafood from your supermarket for this recipe. If frozen, defrost thoroughly before use. Or, if you have more time, put together your own selection of seafood.

1 small red pepper, about 150 g (5 oz)
1 red chilli
50 g (2 oz) blanched almonds, toasted
2-3 garlic cloves, peeled and crushed
30 ml (2 tbsp) red wine vinegar
350 ml (12 fl oz) tomato juice
60 ml (4 tbsp) chopped fresh parsley
salt and pepper
400 g (14 oz) dried spaghetti
450 g (1 lb) mixed prepared cooked seafood, such as prawns, mussels and squid (see left)

1 Preheat the grill to high. Place the pepper and chilli on the grill rack and grill, turning occasionally, until the skins char and blacken. Place in a covered dish, let cool slightly, then peel away the skins. Halve, core and deseed, then put the flesh into a food processor bowl.

2 Add the nuts, garlic, vinegar, tomato juice, half the parsley and seasoning. Blend until almost smooth, then transfer to a saucepan.

3 Cook the pasta in a large pan of boiling salted water until *al dente*.

4 Meanwhile, gently heat the sauce until it reaches simmering point. Add the seafood and simmer for 3-4 minutes or until heated through, stirring frequently. Adjust the seasoning.

5 Drain the cooked spaghetti and toss with the remaining parsley. Serve immediately, topped with the seafood sauce.

NOTE: Remember to wear rubber gloves when handling fresh chillies to prevent skin irritation.

Penne with Olives, Chilli and Anchovy

Serves 4-6
Preparation 10 minutes
Cooking 10 minutes
660-440 calories per serving

If you are lucky enough to have a local delicatessen which has bowls of tasty olives marinating in flavoured oils, buy some to use in this recipe. They are usually far more delicious than olives found in jars or tins in supermarkets and can be much cheaper. Serve this dish accompanied by a crisp leafy salad.

400 g (14 oz) dried penne
salt and pepper
2 garlic cloves, peeled and thinly sliced
50 g (2 oz) can anchovies in olive oil
2.5 ml (½ tsp) dried chilli flakes
30 ml (2 tbsp) chopped fresh parsley
225 g (8 oz) pitted mixed black and green olives
60 ml (4 tbsp) extra-virgin olive oil
30-45 ml (2-3 tbsp) freshly grated Parmesan cheese
extra Parmesan cheese, to serve

1 Bring a large saucepan of salted water to the boil. Add the pasta and cook until *al dente*.

2 Meanwhile, put the sliced garlic in a saucepan with the anchovies and their oil. Add the chilli flakes and cook over a fairly high heat for 2-3 minutes, stirring to break up the anchovies with a wooden spoon; do not allow the garlic to brown. Stir in the parsley and remove from the heat.

3 Transfer the contents of the pan to a food processor and add the olives and olive oil. Process for a few seconds to give a coarse paste. Season with pepper to taste; salt shouldn't be needed.

4 When the pasta is cooked, drain thoroughly, then return to the saucepan. Add the pounded olive mixture and the Parmesan. Toss well and serve immediately, topped with Parmesan shavings.

Thai Stir-fried Noodles with Tofu

Serves 4
Preparation 20 minutes
Cooking 35 minutes
400 calories per serving

This recipe is based on the classic Thai noodle dish *phat thai* which is freshly cooked at street stalls in Thailand and eaten as a snack.

125 g (4 oz) tofu, drained and cut into 2.5 cm (1 inch) cubes
8 shallots, peeled and halved
1 garlic clove, peeled and crushed
2.5 cm (1 inch) piece fresh root ginger, peeled and crushed
30 ml (2 tbsp) sweet soy sauce
5 ml (1 tsp) rice vinegar
225 g (8 oz) rice noodles
30 ml (2 tbsp) sunflower oil
15 g (½ oz) dried shrimp (optional)
1 egg, beaten

25 g (1 oz) bean sprouts

SAUCE
1 dried red chilli, seeded and finely chopped
30 ml (2 tbsp) lemon juice
15 ml (1 tbsp) Thai fish sauce
15 ml (1 tbsp) caster sugar
30 ml (2 tbsp) smooth peanut butter

TO GARNISH
25 g (1 oz) peanuts, chopped and toasted

1 Preheat the oven to 200°C (400°F) Mark 6. Put the tofu and shallots in a small roasting tin. Blend the garlic, ginger, soy sauce, vinegar and 30 ml (2 tbsp) water together. Pour over the tofu and shallots and toss well. Roast near the top of the oven for 30 minutes or until golden.

2 Meanwhile soak the noodles according to the packet instructions. Drain, refresh under cold running water and set aside.

3 For the sauce, place all of the ingredients in a small pan and stir over a gentle heat until the sugar is dissolved. Keep warm.

4 Heat the oil in a wok and stir-fry the dried shrimp, if using, for 1 minute. Add the noodles and egg to the wok and stir over a medium heat for 3 minutes. Add the tofu and shallots, together with any pan juices, and toss to mix.

5 Remove from the heat and stir in the bean sprouts and sauce. Serve at once, sprinkled with the toasted peanuts.

VARIATION
Replace the tofu with 125 g (4 oz) minced pork. Quickly stir-fry the pork shallots, garlic and ginger in a little oil until browned. Stir in the noodles and eggs and stir-fry for 2 minutes, then add the remaining ingredients, cover the pan and heat through.

Pasta with Pepperoni, Red Onion and Pimentos

Serves 4
Preparation 10 minutes
Cooking 20 minutes
615 calories per serving

Lasagnette works well in this simple recipe, but you could use pappardelle or tagliatelle instead if you prefer.

45 ml (3 tbsp) olive oil
2 red onions, peeled and sliced
3 garlic cloves, peeled and sliced
2 canned pimentos, drained and cut into strips
125 g (4 oz) pepperoni sausage, sliced
60 ml (4 tbsp) red wine
400 g (14 oz) can chopped tomatoes
5 ml (1 tsp) sun-dried tomato paste
salt and pepper
350 g (12 oz) dried lasagnette
45 ml (3 tbsp) chopped fresh parsley
75 ml (5 tbsp) freshly grated Parmesan cheese

1 Heat 30 ml (2 tbsp) of the oil in a large frying pan. Add the onions and garlic, and cook for 5 minutes or until softened and golden. Add the pimento strips, and cook for a further minute. Remove the vegetables from the pan with a slotted spoon and set aside.

2 Heat the remaining oil in the pan. Add the pepperoni slices and cook over a high heat until browned and almost crisp. Return the vegetables to the pan and add the wine. Cook over a high heat until the wine is reduced by half. Add the tomatoes and sun-dried tomato paste. Season with salt and pepper. Simmer for 15 minutes.

3 Meanwhile, cook the pasta in a large saucepan of boiling salted water until *al dente*. Drain thoroughly and return the pasta to the pan. Add the vegetable and pepperoni sauce and toss well. Add the parsley and 30 ml (2 tbsp) of the Parmesan; toss again. Serve at once, sprinkled with the remaining Parmesan.

Linguine with Parma Ham and Sun-Dried Tomatoes

Serves 4-6
Preparation 5 minutes
Cooking 10 minutes
1020-680 calories per serving

Illustrated opposite

If you like the distinctive flavour of Parma ham eaten raw as a starter with melon, you will almost certainly enjoy it in cooked dishes too. Here thin strips are quickly fried in olive oil until frazzled – to delicious effect.

400 g (14 oz) dried linguine or fettucini
salt and pepper
30 ml (2 tbsp) olive oil
125 g (4 oz) Parma ham, cut into thin strips
65 g (2½ oz) butter
1 large onion, peeled and chopped
2 garlic cloves, peeled and crushed
50 g (2 oz) sun-dried tomatoes, drained and cut into strips
150 ml (¼ pint) double cream
150 g (5 oz) mascarpone cheese
15-30 ml (1-2 tbsp) chopped fresh marjoram or oregano
30-45 ml (2-3 tbsp) toasted pine nuts (optional)

1 Cook the pasta in a large saucepan of boiling salted water until *al dente*.

2 Meanwhile, heat the oil in a frying pan, add the Parma ham strips and fry quickly for about 1 minute or until frazzled. Using a slotted spoon, remove the ham from the pan and set aside.

3 Add the butter to the frying pan and gently fry the onion, garlic and sun-dried tomatoes for 2 minutes.

4 In a saucepan, gently heat the cream with the mascarpone, stirring until smooth. Season with salt and pepper.

5 Drain the pasta, and while still hot, add to the frying pan and toss to mix. Add the cream mixture, together with half of the Parma ham and half the marjoram or oregano. Toss to mix.

6 Serve at once, topped with the remaining Parma ham, herbs and toasted pine nuts, if using.

VARIATIONS
Use strips of pancetta or smoked streaky bacon instead of Parma ham and cook in the same way. Sautéed sliced mushrooms or asparagus tips also make tasty additions.

Pasta with Mushrooms, Bacon and Leeks

Serves 4-6
Preparation 10 minutes
Cooking About 10 minutes
650-435 calories per serving

A deliciously rich, warming, pasta dish for a cold winter's day. The creamy mushroom and leek sauce can be prepared within the time it takes to cook the pasta.

450 g (1 lb) dried pappardelle, tagliatelle or linguine
salt and pepper
25 g (1 oz) butter
225 g (8 oz) mushrooms, thinly sliced
125 g (4 oz) trimmed leeks, thinly sliced

125 g (4 oz) pancetta or unsmoked streaky bacon, derinded and chopped
1 garlic clove, peeled and crushed
125 g (4 oz) full-fat soft cheese with garlic and herbs
30 ml (2 tbsp) milk or single cream

1 Cook the pasta in a large saucepan of boiling salted water until *al dente*.
2 Meanwhile, melt the butter in a saucepan. Add the mushrooms, leeks, pancetta or bacon and garlic. Fry for 3-4 minutes or until the leeks are tender but still retain some bite, stirring continuously.
3 Lower the heat and stir in the soft cheese and milk or cream until thoroughly mixed. Season with salt and pepper to taste.
4 Drain the pasta thoroughly and toss with the mushroom and leek sauce. Serve at once.

Noodles with Parma Ham and Parmesan Cream

Serves 4
Preparation 10 minutes
Cooking 15 minutes
365 calories per serving

Parma ham adds a distinctive flavour to this simple supper dish, but if you haven't any to hand use thinly sliced cooked ham instead.

225 g (8 oz) dried pappardelle or tagliatelle
salt and pepper
350 g (12 oz) asparagus or French beans, cut into 7.5 cm (3 inch) lengths

125 g (4 oz) trimmed leeks, shredded
50 g (2 oz) Parma ham, chopped
150 ml (¼ pint) single cream
50 g (2 oz) freshly grated Parmesan cheese

1 Cook the pasta in a large pan of boiling salted water until *al dente*.
2 Meanwhile, cook the asparagus or beans in boiling salted water for 7-10 minutes until just tender. Add the leeks and boil for 30 seconds, then drain well.
3 Put the cream in a small pan with half of the grated cheese. Heat until just boiling, stirring. Transfer to a warmed jug.
4 Drain the pasta thoroughly. Toss with the vegetables, ham and remaining cheese. Season with salt and pepper to taste.
5 Serve at once, handing the Parmesan Cream around separately.

Fettucine with Peppered Salami

Serves 4
Preparation 15 minutes
Cooking 10 minutes
795 calories per serving

You need the minimum of ingredients to create this tasty supper dish. Serve it with a crisp leafy salad.

350 g (12 oz) dried fettucine
salt and pepper
25 g (1 oz) butter
125 g (4 oz) shallots, peeled and sliced
125 g (4 oz) brown-cap mushrooms, sliced
275 g (10 oz) peppered salami, skinned and cut into strips

125 g (4 oz) soft cheese with garlic and herbs, such as Boursin
150 ml (¼ pint) single cream
60 ml (4 tbsp) milk
freshly grated Parmesan cheese, to serve (optional)

1 Cook the pasta in a large pan of boiling salted water until *al dente*.
2 Meanwhile, heat the butter in a pan, add the shallots and fry until golden. Add the mushrooms and fry for about 5 minutes until beginning to soften. Add the salami and fry, stirring, for 1-2 minutes.
3 Lower the heat and stir in the soft cheese, cream and milk. Simmer, stirring, for about 2 minutes until piping hot.
4 Drain the pasta and return to the saucepan, pour on the sauce and toss to mix. Adjust the seasoning and serve immediately, sprinkled with a little Parmesan if wished.

Pasta with Bacon, Tomato and Olive Sauce

Serves 4
Preparation 10 minutes
Cooking 10 minutes
720 calories per serving

Vary the herbs in this quick bacon ragù according to taste.

350 g (12 oz) dried pasta, such as vermicelli, spaghetti or penne
salt and pepper
60 ml (4 tbsp) olive oil
2 garlic cloves, peeled and crushed
225 g (8 oz) smoked streaky bacon, derinded and chopped

two 400 g (14 oz) cans chopped tomatoes
125 g (4 oz) black olives, stoned and chopped
60 ml (4 tbsp) chopped fresh basil or marjoram

1 Cook the pasta in a large pan of boiling salted water until *al dente*.
2 Meanwhile, heat 30 ml (2 tbsp) oil in a frying pan, add the garlic and bacon and fry until golden. Stir in the tomatoes, olives and herbs and heat through for 2-3 minutes until piping hot. Season with salt and pepper to taste.
3 Drain the pasta and toss with the remaining oil. Add the bacon sauce and toss well. Serve immediately.

SOUPS WITH PASTA

Pasta and Chick Pea Soup with Rocket Pesto

Serves 6
Preparation 25 minutes
Cooking 1 hour
370 calories per serving

Illustrated on page 41

This soup is similar to a minestrone with its selection of fresh green vegetables, but the pesto sauce is made with peppery rocket, rather than the usual basil. The rocket gives a cleaner taste to the finished soup and adds a vivid splash of green.

45 ml (3 tbsp) olive oil
1 onion, peeled and chopped
2 garlic cloves, peeled and finely chopped
1 small leek, sliced
15 ml (1 tbsp) chopped fresh rosemary
400 g (14 oz) can chick peas
1.2 litres (2 pints) vegetable stock
4 ripe tomatoes, skinned and chopped
1 courgette, diced
125 g (4 oz) shelled peas

125 g (4 oz) French beans, halved
125 g (4 oz) shelled broad beans
50 g (2 oz) dried pastina (small soup pasta)
30 ml (2 tbsp) chopped fresh parsley
salt and pepper

TO SERVE
1 quantity rocket pesto (see page 19)
freshly grated pecorino or Parmesan cheese

1 Heat the oil in a large saucepan, add the onion, garlic, leek and rosemary and fry gently for 10 minutes until softened but not coloured. Add the chick peas with their liquid, the stock and tomatoes. Bring to the boil, cover and simmer for 30 minutes.

2 Add the courgette, peas and beans to the soup. Return to the boil and simmer for a further 10 minutes. Add the pasta and parsley and cook for 6-8 minutes until the pasta is *al dente*. Check the seasoning.

3 Serve topped with a spoonful of rocket pesto and a sprinkling of cheese.

VARIATION
Use borlotti beans instead of chick peas. Replace half the stock with an equal quantity of tomato juice. Substitute the peas with 125 g (4 oz) button mushrooms. Fry the mushrooms in 15 ml (1 tbsp) olive oil and add to the soup with the remaining green vegetables.

Thai Vegetable, Noodle and Tofu Broth

Serves 4
Preparation 20 minutes
Cooking 1¼ hours, including stock
135 calories per serving

The success of this light, delicate soup depends on the quality of the stock, which is used to poach a selection of vegetables and the tofu.

STOCK
1 onion, peeled and roughly chopped
2 carrots, peeled and roughly chopped
2 celery sticks, peeled and roughly chopped
2 garlic cloves, peeled and chopped
2 lemon grass stalks, roughly chopped
15 g (½ oz) fresh root ginger, peeled and roughly chopped
4 kaffir lime leaves
4 coriander roots, scrubbed
5 ml (1 tsp) white peppercorns
5 ml (1 tsp) salt

BROTH
25 g (1 oz) dried black or shiitake mushrooms
30 ml (2 tbsp) dark soy sauce
15 ml (1 tbsp) lemon or lime juice
1 large carrot, peeled and cut into julienne
50 g (2 oz) cauliflower, divided into small florets
50 g (2 oz) baby sweetcorn, halved lengthwise
125 g (4 oz) plain tofu, cut into 2 cm (¾ inch) cubes
50 g (2 oz) dried egg thread noodles

TO SERVE
mint leaves
chilli oil

1 Put all of the stock ingredients in a large saucepan with 1.2 litres (2 pints) water. Bring to the boil, cover and simmer over a gentle heat for 1 hour.

2 Meanwhile, put the dried mushrooms in a bowl, pour on 120 ml (4 fl oz)

boiling water and leave to soak for 30 minutes. Strain and reserve the liquid; chop the mushrooms.

3 Strain the stock into a clean pan and stir in the soy sauce, lemon or lime juice and reserved mushroom liquid. Return to the boil and stir in the prepared vegetables, tofu and soaked mushrooms. Simmer for 5 minutes.

4 Plunge in the noodles and simmer for a further 5-6 minutes until the noodles and vegetables are tender. Serve at once, in warmed soup bowls, scattered with mint leaves and drizzled with a little chilli oil.

VARIATIONS

If you haven't time to prepare the stock, make up the required amount of liquid using a good quality ready-prepared vegetable stock and add 15 ml (1 tbsp) each of lime and lemon juice and a pinch of sugar. Alternatively, use chicken stock instead.

Hearty Bean and Pasta Soup

Serves 6
Preparation 15 minutes, plus soaking
Cooking 2½-3½ hours
250 calories per serving

A simple Tuscan white bean soup with pasta shells, served drizzled with a little green olive oil.

175 g (6 oz) dried haricot beans, soaked overnight in cold water
1.7 litres (3 pints) chicken or vegetable stock
125 g (4 oz) medium pasta shapes, such as orecchiette or shells

60 ml (4 tbsp) olive oil
2 garlic cloves, peeled and crushed
60 ml (4 tbsp) chopped fresh parsley
salt and pepper
extra-virgin olive oil, to serve

1 Drain the beans and place in a large saucepan with the stock. Bring to the boil and boil rapidly for 10 minutes, then lower the heat and simmer, half-covered for 2-2¼ hours or until the beans are tender.

2 Transfer half of the beans and a little of the cooking liquid to a blender or food processor and work to a purée. Return to the pan and stir to mix with the rest of the cooked beans.

3 Stir in the pasta, bring to the boil and simmer gently for 15 minutes or until the pasta is tender. Add a little extra water or stock if the soup is a little too thick.

4 Heat the oil in a small pan and fry the garlic until golden. Stir into the soup with the parsley and season generously with salt and pepper. Serve in warmed soup bowls, drizzling each portion with a little extra olive oil.

NOTE: This soup is suitable for freezing at the end of stage 3.

Minestrone with Pesto

Serves 6-8
Preparation 20 minutes, plus overnight soaking
Cooking about 2-2½ hours
540-400 calories per serving

This classic Italian soup is topped with a pesto sauce and freshly grated pecorino or Parmesan cheese. Serve it as a main course with plenty of good bread, encouraging your guests to add a generous spoonful of the pesto to their soup.

175 g (6 oz) dried haricot, cannellini or flageolet beans, soaked overnight in cold water
salt and pepper
2.3 litres (4 pints) vegetable stock
1 dried red chilli
450 g (1 lb) potatoes, peeled and diced
450 g (1 lb) carrots, peeled and diced
2 large leeks, trimmed and thinly sliced
450 g (1 lb) courgettes, diced
225 g (8 oz) French beans, halved
425 g (15 oz) can chopped tomatoes
125 g (4 oz) dried pastina (small soup pasta)

TO SERVE
1 quantity pesto (see page 19)
50 g (2 oz) pecorino or Parmesan cheese, freshly grated

1 Drain the beans and put them in a large saucepan with enough fresh cold water to cover. Bring to the boil and boil steadily for 10 minutes, then lower the heat and simmer for 1-1½ hours or until the beans are tender, adding salt towards the end of the cooking time. Drain thoroughly.

2 Pour the stock into a large saucepan and add the chilli. Bring to the boil, then add the beans, potatoes, carrots and leeks. Lower the heat, cover and simmer gently for 25 minutes or until the vegetables are really tender.

3 Add the courgettes, French beans, tomatoes and pasta to the soup and season generously with salt and pepper. Re-cover and simmer for a further 10 minutes or until the pasta is just cooked.

4 Serve in warmed large soup plates. Hand the pesto and grated pecorino or Parmesan cheese separately.

VARIATIONS
• Use two 425 g (15 oz) cans beans instead of dried ones. Drain and rinse thoroughly under cold running water. Add to the soup towards the end of stage 3 to heat through.
• If you haven't time to make your own pesto use ready-made pesto instead.
• For a fiery version, serve with Chilli Pesto (see page 19).

Japanese Noodle Broth with Pak Choi and Mooli

Serves 4
Preparation 15 minutes
Cooking 30 minutes
215 calories per serving

Illustrated opposite

125 g (4 oz) flat rice or egg noodles
30 ml (2 tbsp) sunflower oil
1 garlic clove, peeled and sliced
5 ml (1 tsp) grated fresh root ginger
pinch of sugar
3 pak choi, about 350 g (12 oz) total weight, roughly chopped
1.1 litres (2 pints) vegetable stock
30 ml (2 tbsp) miso (see note)
15 ml (1 tbsp) lemon juice
15 ml (1 tbsp) light soy sauce
125 g (4 oz) mooli, sliced
1 packet mustard and cress
15 ml (1 tbsp) chopped fresh coriander

1 Cook the noodles according to the packet instructions. Drain, refresh under cold water, then drain thoroughly; set aside.

2 Heat the oil in a saucepan and fry the garlic, ginger and sugar over a low heat for 2 minutes. Add the pak choi, in a single layer if possible, cover and cook over a low heat for 5 minutes. Add the stock, miso, lemon juice, soy sauce and mooli. Bring to the boil, cover and simmer for 15 minutes.

3 Stir in the rice noodles, mustard and cress, and chopped coriander. Heat

Mooli, the long white radish, is a popular Japanese ingredient and gives this dish a distinctive flavour.

the soup through for 1 minute and serve at once.

NOTE: Miso is a thick paste made from fermented soya beans, used to flavour soups, sauces, etc. It is available from healthfood shops and oriental food stores.

VARIATIONS
• Use another variety of Chinese cabbage in place of pak choi.
• If mooli is unavailable, use thinly sliced turnip instead.

Quick Courgette, Pea and Pasta Soup

Serves 4-6
Preparation 20 minutes
Cooking 30 minutes
315-210 calories per serving

A pretty green soup of grated courgettes, fresh or frozen peas, tiny soup pasta and stock, enriched with soured cream. Serve with crusty bread as a starter or light lunch.

60 ml (4 tbsp) olive or sunflower oil

2 onions, peeled and finely chopped

1.4 litres (2½ pints) hot chicken or vegetable stock

450 g (1 lb) courgettes

450 g (1 lb) fresh peas, shelled, or 175 g (6 oz) frozen peas

125 g (4 oz) dried pastina (small soup pasta)

salt and pepper

squeeze of lemon or lime juice, to taste

30 ml (2 tbsp) chopped fresh chervil

soured cream, to serve

chervil sprigs, to garnish

1 Heat the oil in a large saucepan. Add the onions, cover and cook gently for about 20 minutes until very soft but not coloured, stirring occasionally.

2 Pour in the stock and bring to the boil.

3 Meanwhile trim and grate the courgettes. Add to the boiling stock with the fresh peas if using, and the pasta. Turn down the heat and simmer for 10-15 minutes or until the pasta is tender. Season with salt and pepper and add lemon or lime juice to taste. (If using frozen peas, add them 5 minutes before the end of cooking.)

4 Stir in the chopped chervil. Serve in warmed soup bowls, adding a swirl of soured cream to each portion. Garnish with sprigs of chervil.

Prawn and Scallop Won Ton in a Thai Broth

Serves 6
Preparation 25 minutes, plus pasta
Cooking 35 minutes
275 calories per serving

For this Thai-style soup fresh pasta is used to make seafood parcels, in place of traditional won ton. Classic Thai ingredients are used to prepare a fragrant stock, which is then used to poach the delicious seafood parcels. Serve as a starter.

300 g (10 oz) raw Mediterranean prawns

4 lemon grass stalks, roughly chopped

1 garlic clove, peeled and chopped

2.5 cm (1 inch) piece fresh root ginger, sliced

2 chillies, bruised

4 lime leaves, roughly shredded

4 coriander stalks, bruised

1.5 litres (2½ pints) vegetable stock

225 g (8 oz) cleaned scallops, white part only

2 spring onions, trimmed and finely chopped

grated rind and juice of 1 lime

15 ml (1 tbsp) chopped fresh coriander

salt and pepper

1 quantity fresh saffron pasta dough (see page 10)

15 ml (1 tbsp) Thai fish sauce or light soy sauce

5-10 ml (1-2 tsp) chilli sauce

TO SERVE

a little sesame oil

coriander leaves, to garnish

1 Shell the prawns, placing the heads and shells in a large saucepan. Make a slit down the back of each prawn and remove the dark intestinal vein. Dice the prawns and set aside.

2 To make the broth, add the lemon grass, garlic, ginger, chillies, lime leaves and coriander stalks to the prawn shells. Pour on the stock and bring to the boil. Cover and simmer gently for 30 minutes. Strain the stock and reserve.

3 Dice the scallops and mix with the prawns. Add the spring onions, lime rind, chopped coriander and salt and pepper.

4 Divide the pasta dough into 6 equal pieces. Roll out one piece thinly to a 15 x 30 cm (6 x 12 inch) rectangle and halve lengthwise to give 2 strips. Position 4 small mounds of the seafood filling on one pasta sheet, at equal intervals. Brush the pasta dough around the filling with water and position the

second pasta sheet on top. Press down well around the filling to seal, then stamp out the ravioli, using a fluted pastry cutter. Place on a floured tea-towel. Repeat to make 24 won ton.

5 Return the broth to the boil. Add the lime juice, fish sauce and chilli sauce. Add the won ton, return to a gentle simmer, cover and cook for 3 minutes until the pasta and seafood are cooked. Check the seasoning.

6 Spoon the won ton and broth into warmed bowls, drizzle with a little sesame oil and scatter over a few coriander leaves. Serve at once.

NOTE: For convenience – and to allow the flavours to infuse – prepare the stock and seafood filling ahead. Cover and chill until required.

Pork and Noodle Soup

Serves 6
Preparation 25 minutes
Cooking 35 minutes
300 calories per serving

Don't be put off by the few unusual ingredients in this recipe. Most larger supermarkets now stock a range of ready-prepared sauces which includes Thai fish sauce and red curry paste. You may also find packs of Thai herbs – containing lemon grass and kaffir lime leaves – in the fresh herb section.

225 g (8 oz) minced pork
50 g (2 oz) peanuts or cashew nuts, roughly chopped
4 garlic cloves, peeled and crushed
60 ml (4 tbsp) chopped fresh coriander
salt and pepper
1.7 litres (3 pints) chicken stock
3 lemon grass stalks, finely chopped
6 kaffir lime leaves, or a little grated lime rind

15 ml (1 tbsp) light soy sauce
15 ml (1 tbsp) Thai fish sauce
juice of 2 limes
5 ml (1 tsp) red curry paste or tandoori paste
10 ml (2 tsp) caster sugar
60 ml (4 tbsp) oil
125 g (4 oz) rice noodles or egg noodles
125 g (4 oz) mushrooms, sliced
125 g (4 oz) broccoli florets

1 Put the minced pork in a bowl with the chopped nuts, crushed garlic, half the coriander, and salt and pepper. Mix thoroughly, then shape into approximately 18 walnut-sized balls; knead thoroughly with your hands to help bind the mixture and prevent the meatballs breaking up during cooking.

2 Put the chicken stock into a large saucepan with the lemon grass, lime leaves or grated rind, soy sauce, fish sauce, lime juice, red curry paste and sugar. Bring to the boil, lower the heat, cover and simmer for 20 minutes.

3 Meanwhile, heat 45 ml (3 tbsp) oil in a heavy-based frying pan and fry the meatballs in batches for 4-5 minutes or until golden and cooked through. Set aside.

4 Cook the noodles according to the packet instructions.

5 Meanwhile heat the remaining oil in the frying pan and stir-fry the mushrooms and broccoli for 1-2 minutes. Drain the noodles and add to the pan with the meatballs. Strain the broth and combine with the pork and noodle mixture. Serve at once, garnished with the remaining coriander.

NOTE: To prepare ahead, complete to the end of stage 2 a day ahead. Cool, cover and refrigerate the pork balls and stock separately. Complete as above.

Chicken Soup with Garlic and Parmesan Croûtons

Serves 6
Preparation 20 minutes
Cooking about 1¼ hours
385 calories per serving

Illustrated opposite

A hearty main course soup of chicken, pasta and vegetables with robust garlic and Parmesan croûtons to accompany. There are numerous pastina, or pasta shapes, available for adding to soups – including tiny bows, stars, hoops, alphabet letters etc. Use any one of these, or opt for a slightly larger shape if you prefer.

1 small chicken, weighing about 1 kg (2 lb)
300 ml (½ pint) dry white wine
few peppercorns
1-2 red chillis
2 bay leaves
2 rosemary sprigs
1 celery stalk, roughly chopped
4 carrots, peeled
3 onions, peeled
75 g (3 oz) dried pasta shapes
25 g (1 oz) butter

1 garlic clove, peeled and crushed
30 ml (2 tbsp) chopped fresh parsley
1 cos lettuce, finely shredded
salt and pepper

CROÛTONS
50 g (2 oz) butter, softened
1 garlic clove, peeled and crushed
4 thick slices white bread
45 ml (3 tbsp) freshly grated Parmesan cheese

1 Put the chicken in a saucepan in which it fits snugly. Add the wine, peppercorns, chillis, bay leaves, rosemary and celery. Roughly chop 3 carrots; quarter 2 onions. Add these to the pan with about 900 ml (1½ pints) cold water to almost cover the chicken. Bring to the boil, lower the heat, cover and simmer gently for 1 hour.

2 Leave to cool slightly, then transfer the chicken to a plate and strain the stock. When cool enough to handle remove the chicken from the bone and tear into bite-sized pieces; set aside.

3 Preheat the oven to 200°C (400°F) Mark 6. Return the stock to the pan. Bring back to the boil, add the pasta and cook for 5 minutes.

4 Meanwhile, cut the remaining carrot into fine matchsticks; chop the remaining onion.

5 Melt the butter in a clean pan. Add the onion and garlic and cook for 5 minutes until softened. Add the carrot and cook for 2 minutes. Add the stock and pasta and cook for 5 minutes, then stir in the chicken pieces, lettuce and parsley. Heat gently, stirring, until the lettuce has wilted. Season with salt and pepper to taste.

6 Meanwhile, make the croûtons. Mix together the butter and garlic in a small bowl. Remove the crusts from the bread, then spread with the garlic butter and sprinkle with the Parmesan. Cut into squares and place on a lightly greased baking sheet, spacing them a little apart. Bake in the oven for 8-10 minutes until crisp and golden brown.

7 Serve the chicken soup accompanied by the hot garlic and Parmesan croûtons.

NOTE: For the croûtons, cut thick slices from a whole loaf rather than use ready-sliced bread.

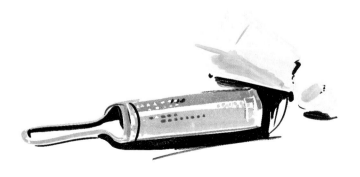

PASTA WITH FISH AND SHELLFISH

Shellfish Pasta with Roasted Cherry Tomatoes

Serves 4-6
Preparation 30 minutes
Cooking 1-1¼ hours
760 - 505 calories per serving

Illustrated on page 51

Roasting tomatoes is a wonderful way of intensifying their flavour. Here the process is successfully applied to cherry tomatoes, to concentrate their natural sweetness. The resulting deep red, soft little tomatoes are tossed into pasta – together with roasted onions and a mixture of seafood. The result tastes as good as it looks!

4 medium-small onions, peeled
450 g (1 lb) cherry tomatoes
75 ml (5 tbsp) extra-virgin olive oil
15 ml (1 tbsp) chopped fresh thyme
salt and pepper
1 kg (2 lb) mussels in shells
12 large raw prawns

450 g (1 lb) squid, cleaned
3-4 garlic cloves, peeled and sliced
175 ml (6 fl oz) dry white wine
few parsley stalks
400 g (14 oz) dried spaghetti
chopped parsley, to garnish

1 Preheat the oven to 200°C (400°F) Mark 6. Cut each onion into 6 wedges, leaving the root end intact. Arrange in one layer in a roasting tin. Halve the cherry tomatoes and arrange cut-side up in the tin. Drizzle over 45 ml (3 tbsp) of the olive oil and sprinkle with the thyme, and salt and pepper. Roast in the oven for 1-1¼ hours until the onions are tender; the tomatoes will be soft.

2 Meanwhile, prepare the shellfish. Scrub the mussels thoroughly under cold running water and pull off the beards. Discard any mussels with cracked or broken shells and those which do not close when tapped firmly. Wash the prawns, but leave them whole. Slice the squid.

3 About 20 minutes before serving, heat 30 ml (2 tbsp) oil in a large saucepan, add the garlic and cook over a medium heat for 1 minute. Add the wine and parsley stalks, bring to the boil and cook for 2 minutes.

4 Add the prawns to the pan and cook gently, covered, for 2 minutes. Add the squid and cook for a further 1-2 minutes until both are cooked. Transfer with a slotted spoon to a plate; set aside.

5 Add the mussels to the pan, cover and cook for 3-4 minutes, shaking the pan frequently, until they open. Drain, reserving the liquid but discarding the garlic and parsley. Discard any mussels which have not opened. Strain the liquor through a muslin-lined sieve and return to the pan with the cooked shellfish.

6 Meanwhile, cook the pasta in a large pan of boiling salted water until almost *al dente*, about 1 minute less than the cooking time. Drain thoroughly, then return to the pan. Add the shellfish and cooking liquor, toss to mix and heat through gently for 1 minute.

7 Add the roasted onion and cherry tomato mixture to the pan and toss lightly. Adjust the seasoning and serve at once, sprinkled with chopped parsley.

VARIATION
Replace the mussels with clams.

Spaghetti with Mussels

Serves 4
Preparation 20 minutes
Cooking 35 minutes
575 calories per serving

1 kg (2 lb) fresh mussels in shells
1 kg (2 lb) flavourful ripe tomatoes, quartered
1 onion, peeled and chopped
4 garlic cloves, peeled
6 basil leaves
150 ml (¼ pint) white wine

450 g (1 lb) dried spaghetti
salt and pepper
30 ml (2 tbsp) olive oil
2 red chillies, halved, seeded and chopped
small basil leaves, to garnish

1 Scrub the mussels thoroughly under cold running water and pull off the 'beards'. Discard any mussels with cracked or broken shells, and those that do not close when sharply tapped with the back of a knife.

This simple dish, spiced with chilli and garlic, relies heavily on the quality of the tomatoes used. Plump, juicy mussels and fragrant basil marry well with the intensely flavoured reduced wine and tomato sauce. There isn't a lot of sauce – any more would overpower the mussels.

2 Put the mussels into a large pan with a cupful of water. Cover with a tight-fitting lid and quickly bring to the boil. Cook for about 3-4 minutes, shaking the pan occasionally, until the mussels have opened. Transfer to a bowl with a slotted spoon, discarding any unopened ones; set aside.

3 Strain the cooking juices through a muslin-lined sieve to remove any sand or grit; reserve.

4 Put the tomatoes and onion in a shallow pan. Crush two of the garlic cloves and add to the pan with the basil. Bring to the boil and simmer for about 20 minutes until the tomatoes start to disintegrate.

5 Press the tomato sauce through a nylon sieve or mouli. Return to the clean pan and pour in the reserved mussel liquid and wine. Bring to the boil and boil rapidly until reduced by about half.

6 Cook the spaghetti in a large pan of boiling salted water until *al dente*.

7 Meanwhile, heat the olive oil in another pan. Chop the other garlic cloves, and add to the pan with the chillies. Cook until golden, then stir in the tomato sauce and mussels. Cover and simmer for 2-3 minutes until heated through. Season with salt and pepper to taste.

8 Drain the spaghetti, holding back 30 ml (2 tbsp) cooking liquid – this will help the sauce to cling to the pasta. Toss the spaghetti with the mussel sauce. Serve immediately, sprinkled with basil leaves.

NOTE: If preferred shell the mussels after cooking at the end of stage 2.

Spaghettini with Creamy Seafood and Saffron Sauce

Serves 4
Preparation 15 minutes, plus soaking
Cooking 20 minutes
880 calories per serving

This superb seafood stew is delicately coloured and flavoured with saffron. Powdered saffron can be used if preferred, but don't resort to turmeric – its flavour is quite incomparable.

450 g (1 lb) mussels in shells
150 ml (¼ pint) dry white wine
2 shallots, peeled and finely chopped
400 g (14 oz) dried spaghettini
salt and pepper
25 g (1 oz) butter
2 garlic cloves, peeled and crushed

10 ml (2 tsp) cornflour
300 ml (½ pint) double cream
2.5 ml (½ tsp) saffron threads
450 g (1 lb) fresh or frozen seafood salad/cocktail, thawed
juice of ½ lemon, to taste
chopped parsley, to garnish

1 Scrub the mussels thoroughly under cold running water and pull off the 'beards'. Leave to soak in a bowl of cold water for 30 minutes. After soaking, tap opened mussels sharply with the back of a knife and discard any that do not close straight away.

2 Drain the mussels and place in a large saucepan with the wine and shallots. Cover tightly and cook, shaking the pan frequently, over a high heat for 5 minutes or until the mussels are open. Discard any unopened ones. Strain and reserve half of the liquid. Set aside the mussels.

3 Cook the pasta in a large pan of boiling salted water until *al dente*.

4 Meanwhile, melt the butter in a saucepan, add the garlic and cook until golden. Stir in the cornflour, then gradually stir in the reserved mussel cooking liquid and cream. Add the saffron, seafood salad and seasoning to taste. Simmer for 2-3 minutes until heated through and slightly thickened.

5 Add the cooked mussels to the sauce, with lemon juice to taste; keep warm.

6 Drain the pasta and toss with the seafood sauce. Serve immediately, garnished with parsley and accompanied by plenty of crusty bread.

Spaghetti with Clams

Serves 4-6
Preparation 15 minutes
Cooking About 8 minutes
685-460 calories per serving

Illustrated opposite

Versions of this classic pasta dish abound, some with tomato, some without, but all with fresh clams, wine, garlic and parsley – the clams should be the main ingredient! Serve with plenty of good bread for soaking up the last of the sauce.

700 g (1½ lb) venus or baby clams in shells
75 ml (5 tbsp) extra-virgin olive oil
3 garlic cloves, peeled and finely chopped
2.5 ml (½ tsp) dried chilli flakes, crushed
100 ml (3½ fl oz) dry white wine

350 g (12 oz) plum tomatoes (or other flavourful tomatoes), skinned, seeded and chopped
salt and pepper
400 g (14 oz) dried spaghetti
30 ml (2 tbsp) chopped fresh parsley
40 g (1½ oz) butter

1 Scrub the clams in cold water, then soak in a bowl of fresh cold water for 10 minutes. Rinse and drain. Discard any which do not close if tapped firmly.
2 Heat the olive oil in a large frying pan (large enough to hold and toss the spaghetti later). Add the garlic and chilli and cook over a medium high heat for 2 minutes; do not let the garlic brown. Stir in the wine and chopped tomatoes.
3 Add the clams to the pan. Season with salt and pepper, stir well and bring to the boil. Cover with a tight-fitting lid and cook for 2-3 minutes to steam open the clams. Remove from the heat; discard any clams which have not opened.
4 Meanwhile, cook the spaghetti in a large pan of boiling salted water until almost *al dente* (about 1 minute less than the cooking time). Drain thoroughly.
5 Return the clam sauce to the heat and stir in the parsley. Add the drained spaghetti and cook for 1 minute; the pasta should finish its cooking in the clam juices. Add the butter, toss lightly and serve at once.

VARIATIONS
Replace the clams with 1 kg (2 lb) fresh mussels in their shells.

Linguine with Seafood and Leek Sauce

Serves 4-6
Preparation 15 minutes
Cooking About 25 minutes
745-495 calories per serving

900 g (2 lb) mussels
30 ml (2 tbsp) olive oil
2 leeks, trimmed and thinly sliced
1 onion, peeled and finely chopped
1 garlic clove, peeled and crushed
large pinch of saffron strands
350 g (12 oz) dried linguine
salt and pepper

200 ml (7 fl oz) dry white wine
150 ml (¼ pint) double cream
45 ml (3 tbsp) chopped fresh parsley
175 g (6 oz) scallops, cleaned (optional)
225 g (8 oz) large cooked peeled prawns
chopped parsley, to garnish

1 Scrub the mussels thoroughly under cold running water and pull off the 'beards'. Discard any mussels with cracked or broken shells, and those that do not close when sharply tapped with the back of a knife.
2 Heat the oil in a large saucepan, add the leeks, onion, garlic and saffron and sauté for 3-4 minutes, stirring all the time. Cover the pan, lower the heat and cook for about 10 minutes until the vegetables are soft.
3 Cook the linguine in a large pan of boiling salted water until *al dente*.
4 Meanwhile, add the wine, cream and parsley to the leek mixture. Bring to the boil and boil for a few minutes to reduce slightly.
5 Add the mussels and scallops, cover tightly and cook for 3-4 minutes, shaking the pan frequently, until the mussels have opened; discard any that remain closed. Add the prawns and heat through gently.
6 Drain the linguine and toss with the seafood sauce. Season with salt and pepper to taste and serve immediately, sprinkled with plenty of parsley.

Tagliatelle with Mussels and Red Pesto

Serves 4-6
Preparation 20 minutes
Cooking About 10 minutes
895-595 calories per serving

The homemade red pesto in this recipe makes a delicious, quick pasta sauce in its own right, tossed into hot pasta ribbons, with or without a little cream or fromage frais. Here it complements freshly steamed mussels. For optimum effect, serve on plain egg pasta to show off the vivid orange colours.

1 kg (2 lb) mussels in shells
1 shallot or small onion, peeled and chopped
90 ml (3 fl oz) dry white wine
30 ml (2 tbsp) chopped fresh parsley
400 g (14 oz) dried ribbon pasta, such as tagliatelle
40 g (1½ oz) butter

RED PESTO
2 garlic cloves, peeled and chopped
25 g (1 oz) walnuts
40 g (1½ oz) basil leaves (from 3 basil plants)
60 ml (4 tbsp) sun-dried tomatoes in oil, finely chopped, plus 30 ml (2 tbsp) oil from the jar
75 ml (5 tbsp) extra-virgin olive oil
30 ml (2 tbsp) pine nuts
75 ml (5 tbsp) freshly grated Parmesan cheese
salt and pepper

TO SERVE
Parmesan cheese

1 First make the red pesto; put the garlic, walnuts and basil in a food processor or blender with the sun-dried tomatoes and their oil, the olive oil and pine nuts. Process until fairly smooth and creamy.

2 Transfer the paste to a bowl and stir in the grated Parmesan. Season with a little salt and plenty of pepper. (Note that the sun-dried tomatoes and cheese are quite salty). Cover and set aside.

3 Scrub the mussels thoroughly under cold running water and pull off the beards. Discard any mussels with cracked or broken shells and those which do not close when tapped firmly.

4 Place the mussels in a large saucepan with the shallot or onion, wine and parsley. Season lightly. Place over a high heat until the liquid comes to the boil, then cover with a tight-fitting lid and cook for 3-4 minutes until the mussels are steamed open. Drain and discard any which have not opened.

5 Shell most of the mussels, then put all of them into a bowl and set aside.

6 Meanwhile, cook the pasta in a large pan of boiling salted water until *al dente*. Drain well.

7 Put the red pesto in a large saucepan and warm gently over a low heat. Add the mussels to the pan and heat *very gently*. Remove from the heat and stir in the butter. Add the pasta and toss to mix. Serve at once, with Parmesan.

NOTE: You can prepare the red pesto up to 1 week in advance and store it in a jar – topped with a layer of olive oil to seal in the flavours.

Pasta with Scallops and Grilled Pepper Purée

Serves 4-6
Preparation 20 minutes
Cooking 35 minutes
780-520 calories per serving

4 red peppers
6 garlic cloves (unpeeled)
450 g (1 lb) shelled medium scallops
75 ml (5 tbsp) extra-virgin olive oil
5 ml (1 tsp) paprika
coarse sea salt and pepper
400 g (14 oz) dried ribbon pasta, such as tagliatelle or pappardelle
45 ml (3 tbsp) chopped fresh parsley
15 ml (1 tbsp) balsamic vinegar or lemon juice
60 ml (4 tbsp) freshly grated Parmesan cheese
parsley sprigs, to garnish

1 Preheat the grill to high. Place the whole peppers and unpeeled garlic cloves on the grill rack. Grill, turning from time to time for about 20 minutes until the peppers are blackened and blistered all over; the garlic cloves will be soft and tender in their papery skins. Allow to cool slightly.

Grilled pepper purée makes a superb pasta sauce – here its sweet smokiness enhances succulent grilled scallops. You could grill a red chilli along with the red peppers for an extra 'kick' if you like. Either way, serve with plenty of bread – preferably Italian olive bread – for soaking up the delicious juices.

2 Holding them over a bowl to catch the juices, peel the peppers, then remove the core and seeds. Peel the garlic. Chop the peppers roughly and put in a food processor with the garlic. Process for a few seconds to give a coarse purée; set aside.

3 Thread the scallops on to wooden skewers and place on a foil-lined grill pan. Brush the scallops with 30 ml (2 tbsp) olive oil. Sprinkle with the paprika and season liberally with sea salt and pepper. Grill for 4-5 minutes, turning once halfway through cooking, until just firm. Remove the scallops from their skewers and slice if large.

4 Cook the pasta in a large pan of boiling salted water until *al dente*.

5 Meanwhile, transfer the pepper purée to a large frying pan. Heat gently, then stir in the scallops and juices from the grill pan. Cook over a gentle heat for 1 minute, then stir in the parsley and balsamic vinegar or lemon juice. Remove from the heat.

6 Drain the pasta thoroughly and return to the pan. Add the remaining 45 ml (3 tbsp) olive oil and toss to mix. Add the sauce and toss lightly. Serve at once, sprinkled with the Parmesan and garnished with parsley.

NOTE: Do not be deterred by the quantity of garlic in this recipe. Grilling whole cloves until soft gives them a mild and creamy flavour.

Orecchiette with Smoked Mussels, Pancetta and Broad Beans

Serves 4
Preparation 20 minutes
Cooking 20 minutes
580 calories per serving

Literally translated, the pasta in this recipe – orecchiette – means 'little ears' which it is supposed to resemble. Don't let this put you off, however, as these little concave cups hold sauce particularly well. Smoked mussels lend a wonderful flavour to this recipe.

175 g (6 oz) shelled fresh or frozen broad beans

salt and pepper

400 g (14 oz) dried orecchiette, or other pasta shapes

60 ml (4 tbsp) olive oil

75 g (3 oz) thinly sliced pancetta, cut into strips

2 shallots, peeled and thinly sliced

2 garlic cloves, peeled and thinly sliced

175 g (6 oz) baby plum or cherry tomatoes, halved lengthwise

105 g (3½ oz) can smoked mussels, drained

45 ml (3 tbsp) chopped fresh parsley

1 Cook the broad beans in boiling salted water for 5-6 minutes until tender. Drain and refresh under cold water. Slip the beans out of their tough outer skins if preferred.

2 Cook the pasta in a large pan of boiling salted water until *al dente*.

3 Meanwhile, heat the oil in a frying pan, add the pancetta and fry over a high heat until crisp. Remove with a slotted spoon and set aside. Add the shallots and garlic to the pan and fry until softened and golden. Add the tomatoes and fry briefly. Stir in the mussels and parsley.

4 Drain the pasta and toss with the mussel sauce and broad beans. Season with salt and pepper to taste. Serve immediately, topped with the crisp-fried pancetta.

NOTE: If pancetta is obtainable, substitute streaky bacon. Baby plum tomatoes are now available from some supermarkets; they have a wonderful flavour and good firm texture, but, if unavailable, use cherry tomatoes instead.

Pasta with Fresh Crab and Ginger

Serves 4-6
Preparation 10 minutes, plus optional pasta and crab preparation
Cooking 8-10 minutes
705-460 calories per serving

For this recipe, you do not necessarily have to deal with a whole crab. Many fishmongers and supermarket fresh fish counters will either dress a crab for you, or sell ready-dressed crab or vacuum-packed fresh crab meat. Note, however, that the quality of ready-prepared crabmeat is variable – seek out a reliable source!

450 g (1 lb) mixed white and brown fresh crab meat, or a 1.5 kg (3 lb) crab, dressed
juice of 2 lemons
90 ml (6 tbsp) extra-virgin olive oil
1 small red onion, peeled and thinly sliced
2 garlic cloves, peeled and crushed
5 ml (1 tsp) grated fresh root ginger
grated rind of 1 lemon
pinch of crushed red chillies
1 quantity fresh linguine (see page 10) or 400 g (14 oz) dried linguine
salt and pepper
60 ml (4 tbsp) chopped fresh parsley

TO SERVE
lemon wedges
extra-virgin olive oil (optional)

1 Flake through the crab meat to ensure there are no pieces of shell remaining, then toss in the lemon juice.
2 Heat the oil in a large frying pan, add the onion, garlic, ginger, lemon rind and chillies and stir-fry for 5 minutes until golden.
3 Cook the pasta in a large pan of boiling salted water until *al dente;* fresh linguine will only take about 1 minute.
4 Meanwhile, add the crab to the frying pan, stir well and heat through for 1-2 minutes.
5 Drain the pasta, reserving 60 ml (4 tbsp) of the cooking water. Add the reserved pasta and water to the crab mixture, together with the parsley. Toss over the heat for 30 seconds. Season with salt and pepper to taste. Serve at once, with lemon wedges, drizzling a little extra olive oil over each portion, if wished.

NOTE: If you buy a fresh crab, ask your fishmonger to open and clean the crab for you. Scoop out all of the brown meat from inside the shell; set aside. Pick out all the white meat from the body section, using a skewer or crab pick. Crack open the legs and claws with crab crackers or a mallet and carefully pick out all of the meat.

Crab-filled Pasta Shells

Serves 4
Preparation 30 minutes
Cooking About 30 minutes
765 calories per serving

Illustrated opposite

This elegant dish is one to reserve for special occasions, though you do not necessarily need to prepare a fresh crab for it (see above). Buy *conchiglioni* – the large dried pasta shells suitable for stuffing, if possible; otherwise use cannelloni tubes.

450 g (1 lb) prepared crabmeat (shell and claws reserved)
300 ml (½ pint) dry white wine
1 lemon grass stalk, grated
60 ml (4 tbsp) crème fraîche (optional)
20 large dried pasta shells (conchiglioni)
25 g (1 oz) butter
1 shallot, peeled and finely chopped
2 red chillies, seeded and finely diced
15 g (½ oz) basil leaves (from 1 plant), finely shredded
salt and pepper
30-45 ml (2-3 tbsp) fresh breadcrumbs
45 ml (3 tbsp) freshly grated Parmesan cheese
olive oil, for drizzling
basil sprigs, to garnish

1 Put the crab claws and shells in a saucepan with the wine, 300 ml (½ pint) water and the lemon grass. Bring to the boil, cover and simmer for 15 minutes to make a stock. Strain, then return to the pan. Boil to reduce by one third. Stir in the crème fraîche, if using. Set aside.
2 Cook the pasta in a large pan of boiling salted water until *al dente*. Drain thoroughly in a colander. Arrange the pasta shells upside-down on a board to dry. Preheat the oven to 220°C (425°F) Mark 7.

3 Melt the butter in a large frying pan. Add the shallot and chillies and sauté over a medium heat for 4-5 minutes to soften; do not brown. Stir in the shredded basil and cook until wilted, then remove from the heat. Add the flaked crabmeat. Mix gently and season with salt and pepper to taste.

4 Mix together the breadcrumbs and Parmesan. Fill the pasta shells with the crab mixture and place in a large baking dish. Pour the reserved stock or sauce around the shells. Sprinkle the breadcrumb mixture over the crab filling and drizzle with olive oil. Cover and cook in the oven for 15 minutes, removing the lid for the last 5 minutes.

5 Transfer the crab-filled shells to warmed serving plates and spoon the sauce or reduced stock around them. Garnish with basil and serve at once.

Pasta with Prawns, Mushrooms and Wine

Serves 4-6
Preparation 30 minutes, plus soaking
Cooking 12-15 minutes
675-450 calories per serving

'Butterflying' prawn tails makes them curl prettily as they cook...and it's very easy to do. This technique also enables the sauce to permeate right through to the prawn flesh. If you need to save time, however, you can omit this stage.

15 g (½ oz) dried porcini mushrooms
16 large raw prawn tails in shells, about 450 g (1 lb) total weight
25 g (1 oz) butter
60 ml (4 tbsp) extra-virgin olive oil
1 onion, peeled and chopped
2 garlic cloves, peeled and crushed
150 ml (¼ pint) dry white wine
400 g (14 oz) dried pasta shapes, such as shells, pipes or twists
salt and pepper
4 tomatoes, skinned, seeded and diced
30 ml (2 tbsp) chopped fresh parsley

1 Put the dried mushrooms in a small bowl and cover with 150 ml (¼ pint) boiling water. Leave to soak for 20 minutes then drain, reserving the liquor, but take care to exclude any grit. Rinse the mushrooms and chop fairly finely.
2 'Butterfly' the prawns by snipping each one lengthwise almost in half from head to tail, leaving the tail end intact. Set aside.
3 Heat the butter and oil in a large frying pan. Add the onion and cook for 5 minutes, stirring frequently, until soft but not browned. Stir in the garlic and cook for a further minute, then add the prawns and mushrooms. Cook, stirring, for a few seconds, then pour in the wine and reserved mushroom liquor. Simmer for 2-3 minutes until the prawns are firm and cooked through.
4 Meanwhile, add the pasta shapes to a large pan of boiling salted water and cook until *al dente*.
5 Using a slotted spoon transfer the prawns to a plate; set aside. Continue cooking the mushroom mixture until the liquid is reduced by half, then stir in the tomatoes. Return the prawns to the pan and season with salt and pepper.
6 Drain the pasta thoroughly and toss with the sauce and chopped parsley. Serve at once.

VARIATION
For a rich, creamy version, add 150 ml (¼ pint) double cream to the pan at stage 5, after removing the prawns. Reduce the liquid by half in the same way. Finish as above.

Stir-fried Orzo with Prawns and Thai Flavourings

Serves 4
Preparation 15 minutes
Cooking 15 minutes
550 calories per serving

225 g (8 oz) orzo pasta
350 g (12 oz) large raw or cooked prawns, shelled
15 ml (1 tbsp) vegetable oil
5 ml (1 tsp) sesame oil
4 shallots, peeled and chopped
1 red pepper, cored, seeded and thinly sliced
6 spring onions, trimmed and sliced
125 g (4 oz) sugar snap peas
125 g (4 oz) creamed coconut, crumbled
20 ml (4 tsp) Thai red curry paste
60 ml (4 tbsp) chopped fresh coriander

1 Cook the pasta in a large pan of boiling salted water until almost *al dente* (about 1 minute less than the cooking time). Drain, refresh under cold water and set aside.
2 If using raw prawns, slit them down the back and remove the black intestinal vein. Rinse under cold water, drain and pat dry with kitchen paper.
3 Heat the vegetable and sesame oils in a wok or large sauté pan. Add the shallots, pepper and spring onions, and stir-fry for 2-3 minutes until softened.

Orzo pasta – also known as puntalette – looks like grains of rice. In this recipe, it is stir-fried with large prawns, vegetables, coconut, coriander and Thai red curry paste. It's an unusual combination, but one that works well.

4 Add the sugar snaps, with the raw prawns if using. Continue to cook for 2-3 minutes, until the prawns have turned pink.

5 Stir in the creamed coconut and red curry paste. As soon as the coconut cream has melted, add 100 ml (3½ fl oz) water, the pasta and cooked prawns if using. Continue cooking and stirring for a further 1-2 minutes until the pasta is heated through.

6 Stir in the chopped coriander and serve immediately.

Prawn and Leek Pasta Shells

Serves 4
Preparation 15 minutes
Cooking About 15 minutes
365 calories per serving

20 conchiglioni (large dried pasta shells for stuffing)
salt and pepper
15 g (½ oz) butter
30 ml (2 tbsp) plain flour
450 ml (¾ pint) milk
25 g (1 oz) Parmesan cheese, freshly grated

10 ml (2 tsp) oil
350 g (12 oz) trimmed leeks, thinly sliced
125 g (4 oz) cooked peeled prawns
10 ml (2 tsp) lemon juice
125 g (4 oz) cottage cheese

1 Cook the pasta in a large pan of boiling salted water until *al dente*. Place upside-down in a colander to drain.

2 Meanwhile melt the butter in a pan, stir in the flour and cook, stirring, for 1 minute. Off the heat, gradually stir in the milk. Bring to the boil, stirring, until the sauce thickens. Simmer for 1-2 minutes. Stir in the Parmesan cheese. Keep warm.

3 Heat the oil in a large frying pan. Add the leeks and cook for 2-3 minutes until soft and golden brown. Stir in the prawns and lemon juice. Sauté for a further 1 minute until the prawns are heated through and excess moisture is driven off. Remove from the heat and stir in the cottage cheese and seasoning to taste.

4 Preheat the grill to high. Drain the pasta shells thoroughly and fill with the leek mixture. Place in a gratin dish and spoon over the Parmesan sauce. Grill until golden brown and bubbling. Serve immediately.

Black Peppercorn Pappardelle with Salmon and Saffron Cream

Serves 4
Preparation 20 minutes, plus pasta
Cooking 15-20 minutes
840 calories per serving

Illustrated opposite

This dish provides a stunning medley of flavours, colours and textures. The peppercorns in the fresh pappardelle soften and lose some of their intensity as the pasta cooks. If you wish to use dried pasta as an alternative, opt for plain dried pappardelle.

150 ml (¼ pint) hot vegetable stock
2.5 ml (½ tsp) saffron threads
225 g (8 oz) shelled broad beans
125 g (4 oz) shelled peas
50 g (2 oz) unsalted butter
2 shallots, peeled and finely chopped
1 small garlic clove, peeled and crushed

90 ml (3 fl oz) dry white wine
150 ml (¼ pint) double cream
30 ml (2 tbsp) chopped fresh dill
350 g (12 oz) skinless salmon fillet
1 quantity fresh black peppercorn pappardelle (see page 11), or 400 g (14 oz) dried pappardelle
salt and pepper

1 Pour the hot stock into a bowl, add the saffron threads and leave to infuse for 10 minutes. Blanch the broad beans in lightly salted boiling water for 1 minute; drain, refresh under cold water and pat dry. Squeeze the beans out of their tough outer skins. Blanch the peas for 1 minute; drain, refresh under cold water and dry well.

2 Melt half the butter in a saucepan, add the shallots and garlic and sauté over a low heat for 5 minutes until softened but not coloured.

3 Add the wine and boil rapidly until reduced to about 15 ml (1 tbsp), then add the infused stock and boil for 3 minutes. Stir in the cream and simmer for a further 4-5 minutes until thickened. Remove from the heat and stir in the dill.

4 Meanwhile, melt the remaining butter in a large heavy-based frying pan. Add the salmon fillet and fry for 3 minutes on each side until golden. Remove from the pan and leave until cool enough to handle, then roughly flake the fish.

5 Pour the saffron cream into the frying pan (used to cook the salmon). Stir in the beans and peas and heat through for 5 minutes.

6 Meanwhile cook the pasta in a large pan of boiling salted water for 1-2 minutes until *al dente*.

7 Drain the pasta, add to the sauce and toss well. Season with salt and pepper to taste and immediately spoon the pappardelle into individual bowls. Top each serving with the flaked fish and serve at once.

Linguine with Clams and Smoked Salmon

Serves 6
Preparation 5 minutes
Cooking About 10 minutes
485 calories per serving

Serve this rich dish as a starter, with a light main course to follow.

450 g (1 lb) dried linguine or spaghetti
salt and pepper
290 g (10 oz) can baby clams in brine, drained
225 g (8 oz) thinly sliced smoked salmon

75 g (3 oz) unsalted butter
1 garlic clove, peeled and crushed
45-60 ml (3-4 tbsp) chopped fresh parsley
30 ml (2 tbsp) lemon juice
freshly grated Parmesan cheese, to serve (optional)

1 Cook the linguine in a large pan of boiling salted water until almost ready, but not quite *al dente* (about 1 minute less than the cooking time).

2 Meanwhile, rinse the clams under cold running water; drain well. Cut the smoked salmon into strips.

3 Drain the cooked pasta. Melt the butter in a large frying pan, add the garlic, parsley and pasta and toss together for 1 minute. Add the lemon juice and pepper to taste.

4 Stir in the clams and smoked salmon and toss over a medium heat for 1-2 minutes or until heated through. Serve at once, sprinkled with a litttle freshly grated Parmesan if desired.

Pasta with Salmon and Dill

Serves 4-6
Preparation 15 minutes
Cooking 18-20 minutes
1000-670 calories per serving

This dish combines the distinctive flavours of fresh and smoked salmon to delicious effect. It is important to add the smoked salmon at the end of cooking in order to preserve its texture and flavour. If preferred, use tagliatelle, linguine, or *paglia e fieno* instead of pasta shells.

300 g (10 oz) fresh salmon fillet, skinned
125 g (4 oz) sliced smoked salmon
40 g (1½ oz) butter
1 onion, peeled and chopped
250 ml (8 fl oz) dry white wine
30 ml (2 tbsp) wholegrain mustard
400 g (14 oz) dried pasta shells
salt and pepper

300 ml (½ pint) extra-thick double cream
30-45 ml (2-3 tbsp) chopped fresh dill

TO GARNISH
dill sprigs
toasted pine nuts, for sprinkling (optional)

1 Cut the fresh salmon fillet into 2.5 cm (1 inch) cubes. Cut the smoked salmon into strips.
2 Melt the butter in a large frying pan. Add the onion and cook over a medium heat for about 7 minutes until soft and golden. Stir in the wine and mustard and bring to the boil. Cook for 5-7 minutes until reduced by about half.
3 Meanwhile, cook the pasta in a large pan of boiling salted water until *al dente*.
4 Add the cream to the sauce and simmer for 1 minute, then lower the heat. Add the fresh salmon and cook gently for 2-3 minutes until firm. Stir in the dill and season with pepper. Remove from the heat.
5 Drain the cooked pasta. Toss with the sauce and smoked salmon strips. Serve at once, garnished with tiny sprigs of dill and sprinkled with toasted pine nuts, if wished.

Fresh Dill Tagliatelle with Smoked Salmon in a Butter Sauce

Serves 4-6
Preparation 20-25 minutes, plus resting
Cooking 2 minutes
970-650 calories per serving

Make this stunning combination of delicate pink smoked salmon with a light butter sauce and ribbons of thinnest homemade pale green pasta for a special occasion. If you haven't time to make your own, buy freshly made pasta from a delicatessen or use dried tagliatelle.

DILL PASTA
300 g (10 oz) type '00' pasta flour
pinch of salt
3 eggs
15 ml (1 tbsp) olive oil
50 g (2 oz) fresh dill sprigs

BUTTER SAUCE
1 shallot, peeled and finely chopped

45 ml (3 tbsp) white wine vinegar
225 g (8 oz) unsalted butter, chilled and cubed
salt and white pepper
squeeze of lemon juice

TO ASSEMBLE
225 g (8 oz) smoked salmon
40 g (1½ oz) butter, melted
dill sprigs and lemon wedges, to garnish

1 To make the pasta, sift the flour and salt into a mound on a clean work surface and make a well in the centre. Place the eggs, oil and dill in a blender or food processor and blend until smooth. Pour into the well and gradually mix the liquid into the flour, using the fingers of one hand, then bring the dough together.
2 On a clean surface, with clean hands, knead the pasta for 5-10 minutes until smooth and elastic. Wrap in cling film and allow to rest at room temperature for at least 30 minutes before rolling out.
3 Meanwhile, cut the smoked salmon into strips; cover and set aside.
4 Using a pasta machine or rolling pin, roll out the pasta dough very thinly in batches. Lay on floured tea-towels and leave to dry for 10 minutes. Cut into tagliatelle and let dry for 15 minutes on floured-tea towels before cooking.
5 To make the butter sauce, put the shallot in a small pan with the vinegar and 45 ml (3 tbsp) water. Bring to the boil and boil until reduced to 30 ml (2 tbsp).

Over a low heat, whisk in the butter, a piece at a time, until creamy and amalgamated: this process shouldn't take too long; do not allow to boil or the sauce will split. Season with salt and pepper and add the lemon juice. Stir the smoked salmon into the butter sauce; keep warm.

6 Bring a large pan of salted water to the boil and add the tagliatelle. Boil rapidly for about 2 minutes until *al dente*, then drain thoroughly. Toss the tagliatelle with the melted butter and divide between 4 warmed serving plates. Top with the smoked salmon in butter sauce. Garnish with dill and lemon wedges. Serve at once.

VARIATIONS
Flavour the pasta and sauce with other herbs, such as chives or parsley instead of dill.

Pasta with Smoked Trout, Peppers and Almonds

Serves 4-6
Preparation 20 minutes
Cooking About 30 minutes
785-525 calories per serving

Trout with almonds is a classic combination. In this dish smoked trout fillets are flaked and tossed with grilled red peppers, almonds and lots of fresh dill. It's a robust dish and needs only a simple salad to offset the richness for a perfect pasta meal. A glass of chilled white wine wouldn't go amiss either!

3 large red peppers
225 g (8 oz) smoked trout fillets
60 ml (4 tbsp) extra-virgin olive oil
75 g (3 oz) flaked almonds
400 g (14 oz) dried pasta bows, shells or pipes

45 ml (3 tbsp) chopped fresh dill
40 g (1½ oz) butter
salt and pepper

TO GARNISH
dill sprigs

1 Preheat the grill to hot. Grill the peppers whole, turning occasionally, until the skins are charred and blistered all over. This will take about 20 minutes. Allow to cool slightly, then over a bowl to catch any juices, remove the skins. Cut the peppers into thin strips, discarding the seeds.
2 Flake the smoked trout fillets. Heat the oil in a large frying pan. Add the flaked almonds and cook over a medium heat for about 3 minutes until lightly browned.
3 Meanwhile, add the pasta shapes to a large pan of boiling salted water and cook until *al dente*.
4 Add the grilled pepper strips and any reserved juices to the almonds. Heat through for 1 minute, then stir in the chopped dill and flaked trout. Heat for 1 minute, then remove from the heat and stir in the butter. Season with salt and pepper to taste.
5 To serve, drain the pasta thoroughly. Add to the smoked trout mixture and toss lightly to mix. Serve immediately, garnished with dill.

Saffron Tagliatelle with Red Mullet and Hot Pepper Sauce

Serves 4
Preparation 20 minutes, plus pasta
Cooking 15 minutes
1110 calories per serving

Illustrated opposite

This recipe has all the robust flavours of a typical Mediterranean fish supper. Firm, sweet, red mullet are enhanced by saffron, garlic, orange and herbs. A sauce of chilli and red pepper paste sets the dish off perfectly for an impressive main course.

25 g (1 oz) butter
1 onion, peeled and thinly sliced
300 ml (½ pint) double cream
5 garlic cloves, peeled and crushed
4 strips of pared orange rind
several sprigs of fresh thyme
2 bay leaves
1 quantity fresh saffron pasta (see page 10), or 400 g (14 oz) fresh or dried tagliatelle
salt and pepper

8 red mullet fillets

PEPPER PASTE
1 large red pepper, cored, seeded and roughly chopped
1 red chilli, seeded and roughly chopped
15 g (½ oz) fresh white breadcrumbs
75 ml (5 tbsp) olive oil

TO GARNISH
thyme sprigs

1 First make the pepper paste. Put the red pepper and chilli in a food processor and work to a paste. Add the breadcrumbs, 15 ml (1 tbsp) of the oil and a little salt and blend until smooth. Gradually blend in the remaining oil to make a paste. Turn into a serving dish.
2 Melt the butter in a frying pan, add the onion and fry gently for 5 minutes.
3 At the same time, put the cream, garlic, orange rind, thyme and bay leaves in a small saucepan. Heat gently for 5 minutes while cooking the pasta.
4 Meanwhile, cook the pasta in a large pan of boiling salted water until *al dente*; fresh pasta will only take 1-2 minutes.
5 Pat the red mullet fillets dry with kitchen paper. Add to the frying pan and fry for 1 minute on each side until cooked through.
6 Drain the pasta and return to the pan. Add the onions, red mullet, cream sauce and seasoning and heat through gently. Serve scattered with thyme sprigs and spoonfuls of the pepper sauce.

VARIATIONS
Other firm textured fish can be used instead of red mullet. Try manageable pieces of filleted, skinned monkfish, halibut or sea bass.

Squid and Pasta Stew

Serves 6
Preparation 10 minutes
Cooking About 50 minutes
470 calories per serving

To save time and effort, buy ready prepared squid 'tubes' for this tasty stew. Serve with plenty of bread to mop up the delicious juices.

1 kg (2 lb) cleaned squid, cut into rings
60 ml (4 tbsp) olive oil
2 garlic cloves, peeled and sliced
30 ml (2 tbsp) chopped fresh parsley
100 ml (3½ fl oz) dry white wine

400 g (14 oz) can chopped tomatoes
15 ml (1 tbsp) tomato purée
5 ml (1 tsp) chopped fresh oregano
salt and pepper
400 g (14 oz) dried fusilli, ondule or other pasta shapes

1 Rinse the squid in cold water and pat dry on kitchen paper. Heat the oil in a sauté pan. Add the garlic and parsley, and sauté until the garlic is golden. Add the squid and cook, stirring, until it is opaque.
2 Add the wine, and allow to bubble for about 2 minutes. Add the tomatoes, tomato purée and oregano. Season generously with pepper and stir well. Bring to a simmer, cover and cook gently for about 40 minutes, until the squid is tender.
3 Add 450 ml (¾ pint) boiling water to the pan; once the mixture is bubbling, add the pasta and salt to taste. Cook, uncovered, for a further 10-12 minutes, or until the pasta is *al dente*. Check the seasoning and serve immediately.

Linguine with Monkfish and Grilled Chillies

Serves 4-6
Preparation 20 minutes
Cooking About 20 minutes
605-405 calories per serving

Firm, white monkfish with capers, garlic, coriander, a little cooling mint and the bite of hot, red chilli peppers makes this an unusual, robust pasta dish. However, it's not as hot as you might imagine from the quantity of chillies! Large chillies are milder than small ones, and their fiery heat is tempered when they are grilled.

450 g (1 lb) monkfish, filleted
6-8 large red chillies
15 g (½ oz) butter
60 ml (4 tbsp) extra-virgin olive oil
1 onion, peeled and chopped
3 garlic cloves, peeled and thinly sliced
400 g (14 oz) dried linguine or capellini
finely grated rind of 1 small lemon

30 ml (2 tbsp) capers, rinsed and drained
45 ml (3 tbsp) chopped fresh coriander
10 ml (2 tsp) chopped fresh mint
15 ml (1 tbsp) balsamic vinegar or lemon juice
salt and pepper
coriander leaves, to garnish

1 Cut the monkfish fillet into thin slices; set aside.
2 Preheat the grill to hot. Grill the whole chillies, turning occasionally, until their skins are blackened and blistered all over; this will take about 10 minutes. Carefully peel away the skins, then slit each chilli open lengthwise and rinse out the seeds under cold running water. Dry on kitchen paper. Cut the flesh lengthwise into thin strips.
3 Heat the butter and oil in a large frying pan. Add the onion and cook over a medium heat for 5 minutes, stirring frequently, until softened but not brown. Stir in the garlic and cook for a further minute.
4 Meanwhile, add the pasta to a large pan of boiling salted water and cook until *al dente*.
5 Increase the heat under the frying pan to medium high. Add the monkfish and cook, stirring, for 3-4 minutes until firm and opaque. Add the chilli strips, lemon rind and capers. Remove from the heat and stir in the coriander, mint and balsamic vinegar or lemon juice. Season with salt and pepper to taste.
6 Drain the pasta, add to the sauce and toss lightly to mix. Serve at once, garnished with coriander leaves.

VARIATION
Substitute 350 g (12 oz) peeled prawns for the monkfish reducing the cooking as follows: Do not increase the heat when adding the prawns and heat for only 1 minute before adding the chillies and lemon zest. Continue as above.

Smoked Haddock Stuffed Pasta Shells

Serves 4
Preparation 25 minutes
Cooking 35 minutes
540 calories per serving

350 g (12 oz) undyed smoked haddock
300 ml (½ pint) milk
40 g (1½ oz) butter
4 medium leeks, trimmed and thinly sliced
45 ml (3 tbsp) plain flour

salt and pepper
30 ml (2 tbsp) fresh chopped parsley
20 large pasta shells
45 ml (3 tbsp) fresh breadcrumbs
45 ml (3 tbsp) freshly grated Parmesan cheese

1 Preheat the oven to 150°C (300°F) Mark 2. Put the smoked haddock in a shallow ovenproof dish and pour on the milk. Cover and bake in the oven for about 15 minutes until firm.
2 Remove the fish from the oven and leave until cool enough to handle. Increase the oven setting to 220°C (425°F) Mark 7. Drain the haddock, reserving the milk. Flake the fish, discarding any bones and skin.
3 Melt half of the butter in a pan, add the leeks and cook until soft. Add the flour and cook, stirring, for 1 minute, then add the reserved milk, stirring over

Giant pasta shells are stuffed with a creamy mixture of smoked haddock and leeks, and finished with a crunchy breadcrumb topping. It's worth searching out these shells – called *conchiglioni* – in Italian delicatessens, as they're easy to use and look great! If you aren't able to find any, however, you can use cannelloni tubes instead.

the heat, until thickened. Season with salt and pepper to taste, and stir in the parsley. Leave to cool.

4 Cook the pasta shells in a large pan of boiling salted water until *al dente*. Arrange upside-down in a colander to drain.

5 Add the haddock to the sauce and mix gently. Fill the pasta shells with the haddock mixture. Place them in a greased ovenproof dish.

6 Mix together the breadcrumbs and Parmesan cheese and sprinkle over the filling. Dot with the remaining butter. Cover the dish with foil and cook in the oven for 15 minutes, uncovering for the last 5 minutes to brown the crumbs. Serve immediately, with a crisp salad.

Smoked Fish Raviolini in a Cream Sauce

Serves 4-6
Preparation 30 minutes, plus pasta
Cooking About 20 minutes
970-650 calories per serving

These fluted semi-circular pasta pockets are filled with a smoked fish, parsley and ricotta stuffing and served with a creamy sauce dotted with peas. The recipe suggests a plain egg pasta, but use spinach pasta if you prefer.

RAVIOLINI
1 quantity fresh pasta dough (see page 10)

FILLING
575 g (1¼ lb) smoked haddock fillet
15 ml (1 tbsp) olive oil
15 g (½ oz) butter
1 small onion, peeled and finely chopped
125 g (4 oz) ricotta cheese (if available), or cream cheese
2 egg yolks

30 ml (2 tbsp) chopped fresh parsley

SAUCE
15 g (½ oz) butter
125 g (4 oz) frozen peas
300 ml (½ pint) extra-thick double cream
75 ml (5 tbsp) freshly grated Parmesan cheese
salt and pepper

TO FINISH
30 ml (2 tbsp) snipped chives

1 Wrap the fresh pasta dough in cling film and leave to rest while preparing the filling.

2 To make the filling, preheat the grill to medium-high. Brush the fish all over with the olive oil and grill, skin-side up, without turning, for 5-10 minutes until the flesh is firm and opaque. The exact cooking time will depend on the thickness of the fillet. When cool enough to handle, remove the skin and any bones. Flake the flesh and place in a bowl.

3 Meanwhile, melt the butter in a small frying pan. Add the onion and cook over a medium heat for about 5 minutes until soft but not browned. Add to the fish with the ricotta or cream cheese, egg yolks and parsley. Mix well with a fork and season with pepper; salt should not be necessary. Set aside.

4 Roll out half of the pasta dough as thinly as possible. Using a metal 7.5 cm (3 inch) round fluted cutter, stamp out rounds of dough. Divide half of the filling between the pasta rounds. Brush the edges of the dough with a little water and fold each in half to form semi-circular pockets. Press the edges lightly to seal. Repeat with the remaining pasta dough and filling. You should be able to make about 60 raviolini.

5 To make the sauce, melt the butter in a frying pan, add the peas and cook on a medium heat for 3 minutes. Stir in the cream and bring to the boil. Remove from the heat.

6 Meanwhile, cook the raviolini in batches in a large pan of boiling salted water for 2-3 minutes until *al dente*. Drain thoroughly and transfer to warmed serving plates.

7 Stir the Parmesan into the sauce and season to taste. Pour over the raviolini and toss gently. Serve at once, sprinkled with chives.

Bucatini Siciliana

Serves 6
Preparation 30 minutes
Cooking 40 minutes
840 calories per serving

Illustrated opposite

This pasta recipe is based on Sicily's best-known dish, *pasta con le sarde*, which originates from the capital, Palermo. Traditionally, it is quite dry, with an overall sweet and sour flavour, but this is a moister version with a rich tomato sauce.

50 g (2 oz) raisins
50 g (2 oz) sultanas
90 ml (6 tbsp) olive oil
2 fennel bulbs, roughly chopped
175 g (6 oz) shallots or onions, peeled and roughly chopped
two 400 g (14 oz) cans chopped tomatoes
4 garlic cloves, peeled and crushed
150 ml (¼ pint) red wine
150 ml (¼ pint) vegetable stock
45 ml (3 tbsp) tomato purée
15 ml (1 tbsp) caster sugar
salt and pepper

12 fresh sardines, cleaned and filleted
lemon juice and olive oil, for basting
275 g (10 oz) bucatini or spaghetti
125 g (4 oz) pine nuts
125 g (4 oz) fresh white breadcrumbs
30 ml (2 tbsp) chopped fresh parsley

TO GARNISH
lemon wedges
parsley sprigs

1 Soak the raisins and sultanas in just enough water to cover for about 1 hour, then drain.

2 Heat 30 ml (2 tbsp) olive oil in a large, heavy-based saucepan. Add the fennel and shallots and cook gently for about 5 minutes, stirring frequently.

3 Add the chopped tomatoes and half of the garlic. Slowly bring to the boil, then simmer gently for about 10 minutes.

4 Add the raisins and sultanas, then the wine, stock, tomato purée, sugar and seasoning. Simmer for 30 minutes, stirring occasionally.

5 In the meantime, preheat the grill. Lay the sardines on the grill rack and drizzle over a little lemon juice and olive oil. Grill for about 5 minutes each side, basting frequently.

6 Meanwhile, cook the bucatini or spaghetti in a large pan of boiling salted water until *al dente*.

7 Meanwhile, heat the remaining oil in a frying pan. Add the pine nuts and fry until they just begin to colour. Add the remaining garlic and the breadcrumbs. Fry, stirring, until the breadcrumbs begin to crisp and turn golden brown. Toss in the parsley.

8 Drain the pasta thoroughly and return to the pan. Add the tomato sauce and toss to mix. Spoon into a large serving dish and sprinkle with the breadcrumb mixture. Garnish the grilled sardines with lemon wedges and parsley, and serve with the pasta.

NOTE: Bucatini is the traditional pasta for this recipe. It is a long, hollow pasta, slightly thicker than spaghetti, available from good delicatessens and larger supermarkets. If unobtainable, use spaghetti instead.

Smoked Haddock, Leek and Pasta Gratin

Serves 8
Preparation 40 minutes
Cooking 40-45 minutes
530 calories per serving

Serve this tasty gratin accompanied by a crisp mixed salad. A 'red salad' of radicchio, red chicory and red onion would be perfect.

900 g (2 lb) smoked haddock fillet
750 ml (1¼ pints) milk
125 g (4 oz) butter
900 g (2 lb) trimmed leeks, sliced
salt and pepper
150 ml (¼ pint) double cream
225 g (8 oz) cooked peeled prawns
125 g (4 oz) small pasta shapes, such as penne or shells

10 ml (2 tsp) oil
50 g (2 oz) plain white flour
15 ml (1 tbsp) Dijon mustard
30 ml (2 tbsp) chopped fresh parsley
125 g (4 oz) Cheddar cheese, grated
2 egg whites

1 Preheat the oven to 200°C (400°F) Mark 6. Place the fish in a large frying pan. Pour over about 600 ml (1 pint) milk. Slowly bring to a simmer, cover and simmer gently for 10-12 minutes or until tender. Remove the fish from the milk and allow to cool slightly. Strain the milk into a jug; reserve. Flake the fish into a bowl, discarding the skin and any bones.

2 Melt half the butter in a pan. Add the leeks and cook for 10 minutes or until very soft but not brown. Season with salt and pepper. Stir in the cream, then add to the haddock with the prawns.

3 Cook the pasta in a large pan of boiling salted water until *al dente*. Drain, then toss with the oil.

4 Melt the remaining butter in a pan. Off the heat, stir in the flour, then gradually whisk in the reserved poaching liquid and remaining milk. Bring to the boil, stirring constantly, until smooth and thickened. Cook, stirring, for 2 minutes, then remove from the heat and stir in the mustard, parsley and half of the cheese.

5 Toss the pasta with the leek and fish mixture and place in one 3.4 litre (6 pint) or two 2 litre (3½ pint) ovenproof dishes. Whisk the egg whites until they stand in stiff peaks. Gently fold into the cheese sauce, then pour over the leek and pasta mixture.

6 Sprinkle with the remaining cheese and cook in the oven for about 40-45 minutes or until golden brown.

Seafood and Mushroom Lasagne

Serves 6
Preparation 30 minutes
Cooking 50 minutes
540 calories per serving

30 ml (2 tbsp) olive oil
65 g (2½ oz) butter
1 onion, peeled and finely chopped
450 g (1 lb) button mushrooms, thinly sliced
salt and pepper
4 plum tomatoes, skinned, seeded and roughly chopped
350 g (12 oz) haddock or cod fillet

750 ml (1¼ pints) fish stock
225 g (8 oz) dried lasagne verde
40 g (1½ oz) plain flour
75 g (3 oz) Cheddar cheese, grated
150 ml (¼ pint) double cream
225 g (8 oz) cooked peeled prawns, roughly chopped
30 ml (2 tbsp) chopped fresh parsley

1 Heat the oil and 25 g (1 oz) of the butter in a pan, add the onion and cook until soft. Add the mushrooms and cook over a high heat until tender and all excess moisture has evaporated. Season with salt and pepper to taste. Leave to cool, then stir in the chopped tomatoes.

2 Preheat the oven to 180°C (350°F) Mark 4. Put the haddock or cod fillet in a shallow pan and pour on the fish stock to cover. Bring to a simmer and poach for 5 minutes until barely tender. Remove with a fish slice, reserving the stock. When cool enough to handle, flake the fish.

As a welcome change from the traditional meat-based lasagne, layers of spinach pasta are interleaved with a rich haddock, prawn and mushroom filling in a creamy béchamel sauce. Serve accompanied by a crisp leafy salad.

3 Cook the lasagne in a large pan of boiling salted water according to packet instructions. Drain and lay on a clean tea-towel to dry.

4 To make the sauce, melt the remaining butter in a pan, add the flour and cook for 30 seconds. Gradually pour in the reserved stock, stirring, and cook, stirring, until thickened and smooth. Simmer for 1-2 minutes. Stir in 50 g (2 oz) of the cheese, the cream and seasoning to taste. Leave to cool.

5 Spread a thin layer of sauce over the base of a greased ovenproof dish. Set aside a further 150 ml (¼ pint) of sauce for the topping. Add the prawns and flaked fish to the rest of the sauce, with the mushrooms and parsley. Check the seasoning.

6 Place a layer of lasagne in the base of the dish. Cover with half of the seafood filling. Repeat the layers, then cover with a layer of lasagne. Spread the reserved sauce over the top, and sprinkle with the remaining cheese. Bake for about 50 minutes, until golden brown.

Tuna and Roasted Pepper Pasta Roll

Serves 4
Preparation 30 minutes
Cooking 15-20 minutes
740 calories per serving

This dish is a 'Swiss roll' version of cannelloni – sheets of fresh pasta are spread with a tuna stuffing, then rolled up and sliced to reveal the pretty spiral effect. A béchamel sauce, flavoured with sun-dried tomato paste and Parmesan cheese, is the perfect complement.

2 large red peppers, quartered, cored and seeded

two 200 g (7 oz) cans tuna, drained

100 g (3½ oz) fresh white breadcrumbs

45 ml (3 tbsp) capers in wine vinegar, rinsed, drained and chopped

4 canned anchovies in oil, drained and chopped

30 ml (2 tbsp) olive oil

2 egg yolks

100 g (3½ oz) ricotta cheese

salt and pepper

8 sheets fresh or dried lasagne

SAUCE

20 g (¾ oz) butter

20 g (¾ oz) flour

450 ml (¾ pint) milk

30 ml (2 tbsp) sun-dried tomato paste

30 ml (2 tbsp) freshly grated Parmesan cheese

TO FINISH

30 ml (2 tbsp) chopped fresh parsley

1 Preheat the oven to 200°C (400°F) Mark 6. Preheat the grill to high. Place the pepper quarters on the grill rack, skin-side up, and grill until the skin is blackened. Leave to cool in a covered bowl, then peel away the skins. Chop the peppers finely.

2 Flake the tuna fish in a bowl, then add the breadcrumbs and chopped peppers. Add the capers, anchovies, olive oil, egg yolks and ricotta cheese. Stir well and season to taste, remembering that the anchovies are quite salty.

3 Cook the lasagne in a large pan of boiling salted water until *al dente*. Drain well and lay on a clean tea-towel to dry.

4 Divide the tuna filling between the pasta sheets, spreading it evenly, but leaving a 3 mm (⅛ inch) border around the edges. Roll up each sheet, Swiss-roll style, then slice each roll on the diagonal into four. Lay the rolls, slightly overlapping, in a greased ovenproof dish. Cover and bake in the oven for 15-20 minutes.

5 Meanwhile, make the sauce. Melt the butter in a pan, add the flour and cook for 1 minute. Gradually stir in the milk, and cook, stirring, until thickened. Allow to simmer for 2-3 minutes. Remove from the heat and stir in the sun-dried tomato paste, Parmesan and seasoning to taste. Keep warm.

6 To serve, pour the sauce over the tuna roll slices and sprinkle with the chopped parsley.

PASTA WITH MEAT

Provençal Chicken Bake

Serves 8
Preparation 30 minutes
Cooking 1¾ hours
515 calories per serving

This tasty pasta bake can be prepared ahead, making it perfect for a midweek supper. If you are cooking for 4 people, simple freeze half (at the end of stage 5) for another occasion.

45 ml (3 tbsp) olive oil
225 g (8 oz) onions, peeled and roughly chopped
2 garlic cloves, peeled and crushed
pinch of saffron strands (optional)
15 ml (1 tbsp) dried thyme
150 ml (¼ pint) dry white vermouth or white wine
two 400 g (14 oz) cans chopped tomatoes
550 g (1¼ lb) passata
salt and pepper

15 ml (1 tbsp) caster sugar
225 g (8 oz) dried pasta shells
700 g (1½ lb) skinless chicken breast fillets or boned thighs
25 g (1 oz) butter
25 g (1 oz) plain white flour
450 ml (¾ pint) milk
200 g (7 oz) full-fat soft cheese
50 g (2 oz) stoned black olives
75 ml (5 tbsp) pesto
basil sprigs, to garnish

1 Preheat the oven to 200°C (400°F) Mark 6. Heat 15 ml (1 tbsp) olive oil in a large saucepan, and add the onions, garlic, saffron if using, and thyme. Cook for 1-2 minutes, then pour in the dry vermouth or wine and allow to bubble for 2-3 minutes. Add the tomatoes, passata, seasoning and sugar. Bring to the boil and simmer for 15-20 minutes or until reduced by one third.

2 Meanwhile, cook the pasta in a large saucepan of boiling salted water until *al dente*. Drain, refresh under cold running water and set aside.

3 Cut the chicken into chunks and place in a roasting tin. Drizzle over the remaining olive oil and season with salt and pepper. Cover with foil and cook in the oven for 10-15 minutes or until just tender; do not overcook.

4 Melt the butter in a heavy-based saucepan. Stir in the flour and cook, stirring, for 1 minute, then gradually add the milk, whisking until smooth. Bring to the boil and simmer for a further 5-10 minutes, stirring occasionally. Remove from heat and whisk in the full-fat cheese; season with salt and pepper to taste.

5 Mix together the chicken, pasta, olives and tomato sauce. Spoon into a 3.4 litre (6 pint) ovenproof dish which is about 4 cm (1½ inches) deep. Lightly stir the pesto into the white sauce, to create a marbled effect. Spoon the white sauce over the chicken mixture.

6 Bake in the oven for 30-35 minutes or until golden and heated through. Serve immediately garnished with basil sprigs.

Golden Chicken Lasagne

Serves 6
Preparation 40 minutes
Cooking About 2 hours
990 calories per serving

Illustrated on page 75

An ideal dish to prepare ahead and freeze (at the end of stage 6).

1.4 kg (3 lb) oven-ready chicken
300 ml (½ pint) white wine
1 onion, peeled
handful of leek trimmings
1 celery stick
1 bay leaf
6 peppercorns
salt and pepper
200 g (7 oz) dried lasagne
150 g (5 oz) butter

1 garlic clove, peeled and crushed
450 g (1 lb) trimmed leeks, thickly sliced
90 g (3½ oz) plain white flour
50 g (2 oz) Cheddar cheese, grated
175 g (6 oz) Gruyère cheese, grated
300 ml (½ pint) single cream
60 ml (4 tbsp) freshly grated Parmesan cheese
45 ml (3 tbsp) pine nuts

1 Put the chicken in a saucepan in which it fits snugly. Add half the wine, the onion, leek trimmings, celery, bay leaf, peppercorns and 5 ml (1 tsp) salt. Pour on sufficient cold water to cover. Bring to the boil, cover and simmer for 45 minutes - 1 hour, until tender. Leave until cool enough to handle.

2 Remove the chicken from the stock and cut into bite-sized pieces,

discarding the skin and bones. Reduce the stock by boiling if necessary to about 1 litre (1¾ pints). Strain the stock and skim off the fat.

3 Preheat the oven to 200°C (400°F) Mark 6. Cook the lasagne according to the packet instructions. (Even if using no-cook lasagne we recommend that you boil it for about 7 minutes.)

4 Heat 50 g (2 oz) butter in a saucepan. Add the garlic and leeks and fry for about 10 minutes; remove with a slotted spoon.

5 Add the remaining butter to the pan and heat until melted. Stir in the flour and cook, stirring, for 1 minute. Off the heat, gradually whisk in the reserved 1 litre (1¾ pints) stock and remaining wine. Bring to the boil and cook, stirring, for 4-5 minutes. Off the heat, stir in the Cheddar cheese and two thirds of the Gruyère. Stir in the cream and season liberally with salt and pepper.

6 Spoon a little of the sauce over the base of a 3 litre (5¼ pint) shallow ovenproof dish. Cover with a layer of pasta, followed by chicken, leeks, a sprinkling of Parmesan and a little sauce. Continue layering in this way, finishing with pasta and sauce. Sprinkle over the remaining Gruyère, the Parmesan and pine nuts.

7 Bake in the oven for 45-50 minutes. Leave at room temperature for 10 minutes before serving.

VARIATION
Alternatively, you can use 450 g (1 lb) cooked boneless chicken or turkey. Make the sauce with the wine and chicken stock.

Pasta with Chicken and Niçoise Sauce

Serves 4-6
Preparation 10 minutes
Cooking About 20 minutes
640-425 calories per serving

Although this isn't a traditional Provençal recipe, it has many of the flavours associated with that region of France – including thyme, olives, tomatoes, courgettes and, of course, garlic. If you're making this during the summer use fully ripe, fresh red tomatoes, rather than open a can...but avoid flavourless tomatoes – they simply will not do!

2 chicken breast fillets, skinned
45 ml (3 tbsp) virgin olive oil
2 shallots or 1 onion, peeled and finely chopped
2 garlic cloves, peeled and finely chopped
1 hot red chilli, chopped
2 fresh thyme sprigs
425 g (15 oz) can chopped tomatoes

generous dash of red wine
450 g (1 lb) dried pappardelle or tagliatelle
2 small courgettes, roughly chopped (optional)
handful of black and green olives
15 ml (1 tbsp) capers (optional)
salt and pepper
chopped fresh parsley, to garnish

1 Cut the chicken into bite-sized pieces.

2 Heat the olive oil in a large saucepan. Add the chicken and cook over a high heat until browned all over; remove from the pan and set aside. Add the shallots or onion, garlic and chilli and cook for a few minutes until softened.

3 Return the chicken to the pan and add the thyme, tomatoes and wine. Bring to the boil, lower the heat and simmer for about 15 minutes until the chicken is cooked through.

4 Meanwhile, add the pasta to a large pan of boiling salted water and cook until *al dente*.

5 Add the courgettes and olives to the sauce, with the capers if using. Season with salt and pepper to taste. Simmer for 5 minutes or until the courgettes are cooked but still retain some bite.

6 Drain the pasta thoroughly in a colander. Serve topped with the sauce and garnished with plenty of chopped parsley.

Linguine with Chicken Livers and Vermouth

Serves 4
Preparation 10 minutes
Cooking 12 minutes
830 calories per serving

Illustrated opposite

Serve this rich, sustaining dish accompanied by a salad, or steamed green vegetable.

700 g (1½ lb) chicken livers
400 g (14 oz) dried linguine
salt and pepper
45 ml (3 tbsp) vegetable oil
6 spring onions, trimmed and sliced

5 ml (1 tsp) cornflour
150 ml (¼ pint) dry vermouth
30 ml (2 tbsp) chopped fresh sage
50 g (2 oz) butter, cubed
sage sprigs, to garnish

1 Trim any fat and white membrane from the chicken livers. Rinse the livers and pat dry with kitchen paper. Cut into smaller pieces.
2 Cook the pasta in a large pan of boiling salted water until *al dente*.
3 Meanwhile, heat the oil in a frying pan until smoking. Add the spring onions, followed by the chicken livers. Fry, stirring, for about 2 minutes until the livers are evenly browned, then sprinkle with the cornflour and stir in. Pour over the vermouth, add the chopped sage, cover and cook for 2 minutes. Season with salt and pepper to taste.
4 Drain the pasta thoroughly, toss with the butter and pile into a warmed serving dish. Pour over the chicken liver sauce and serve immediately, garnished with sage sprigs.

Tagliatelle with Chicken and Courgettes

Serves 4
Preparation 15 minutes
Cooking About 35 minutes
640 calories per serving

Buttery chicken is flavoured with garlic, ginger and chilli and tossed into pasta ribbons with melting courgettes and fresh herbs. Serve the dish on its own or accompanied by a crisp, mixed leaf salad – such as rocket and chicory, or radicchio and frisée – tossed in a light, creamy dressing.

4 boneless chicken breasts, skinned
4 cm (1½ inch) piece fresh root ginger, peeled and grated
3 garlic cloves, peeled and finely chopped
3 red chillies, seeded and chopped
65 g (2½ oz) butter

coarse sea salt and pepper
2 small courgettes, thinly sliced
45 ml (3 tbsp) chopped fresh coriander or tarragon
15 ml (1 tbsp) chopped fresh parsley
400 g (14 oz) fresh or dried tagliatelle

1 Preheat the oven to 190°C (375°F) Mark 5. Arrange the chicken breasts in one layer on a large piece of foil and sprinkle with the ginger, garlic and chillies. Dot with 25 g (1 oz) of the butter and season with salt and pepper.
2 Wrap the foil tightly to form a parcel and place on a baking sheet. Bake in the oven for 30 minutes or until the chicken is tender and cooked through.
3 Meanwhile, melt the remaining butter in a large frying pan. Add the courgettes and cook over a medium heat, stirring frequently, for 4-5 minutes until tender and just beginning to brown. Stir in the herbs and cook briefly. Remove from the heat.
4 About 5 minutes before the chicken will be ready, cook the pasta in a large pan of boiling salted water until *al dente*.
5 When the chicken is cooked, carefully lift out, retaining the juices in the foil parcel. Cut the chicken into slices or cubes and return to the foil.
6 Drain the pasta and return to the pan. Add the chicken with its juices and the courgettes, butter and herbs. Toss lightly to mix. Adjust the seasoning to taste and serve at once.

Tagliatelle with Chicken and Mushrooms

Serves 4-6
Preparation 10 minutes
Cooking About 50 minutes
570-380 calories per serving

For this substantial dish, cooked chicken is added to a rich mushroom sauce and tossed with pasta and parsley. Dried mushrooms give the sauce an added depth of flavour; you can buy these from delicatessens and larger supermarkets.

15 g (½ oz) dried porcini or cep mushrooms
15 ml (2 tbsp) olive oil
2 shallots, peeled and chopped
1 carrot, peeled and chopped
1 celery stick, chopped
2 garlic cloves, peeled and crushed
700 g (1½ lb) chestnut mushrooms, roughly chopped
150 ml (¼ pint) chicken stock
1 bay leaf
salt and pepper
350 g (12 oz) cooked chicken, thinly sliced
400 g (14 oz) dried tagliatelle
30 ml (2 tbsp) chopped fresh parsley
30 ml (2 tbsp) crème fraîche (optional)

TO SERVE
freshly grated Parmesan cheese

1 Soak the dried mushrooms in 150 ml (¼ pint) boiling water to cover for 30 minutes. Drain, reserving the liquid. Rinse the mushrooms well, chop them roughly and set aside. Strain the liquid through a fine sieve to remove any grit.
2 Heat the oil in a large pan. Add the shallots, carrot, celery and garlic, and cook gently for about 5 minutes until softened. Add the soaked dried mushrooms and cook for a further 5 minutes, then add the fresh mushrooms. Cook, stirring, for a further 10 minutes.
3 Pour in the stock, reserved liquid and bay leaf. Season with salt and pepper, bring to the boil, lower the heat and simmer, covered, for about 30 minutes.
4 Cook the pasta in a large pan of boiling salted water until al dente.
5 Meanwhile, add the chicken to the mushrooms and cook, uncovered, for a further 5-10 minutes, stirring occasionally. Add the parsley and crème fraîche if using, then check the seasoning.
6 Drain the pasta well, return to the pan, and add the chicken and mushroom sauce. Toss well to mix. Serve immediately, with Parmesan cheese.

Egg Noodles with Stir-fried Chicken and Vegetables

Serves 2
Preparation 10 minutes
Cooking About 10 minutes
730 calories per serving

Vary the vegetable content of this dish according to what you have to hand, but aim to keep a good balance of texture, colour and flavour. Canned sliced bamboo shoots and water chestnuts make good additions too.

1 chicken breast fillet, skinned
1 red pepper, cored and seeded
4 spring onions, trimmed
2 carrots, peeled
250 g (8.8 oz) packet thin egg noodles
about 30 ml (2 tbsp) vegetable oil
2.5 cm (1 inch) piece fresh root ginger, peeled and finely chopped (optional)
1 garlic clove, peeled and finely chopped
125 g (4 oz) shiitake or button mushrooms, halved
few beansprouts (optional)
45 ml (3 tbsp) hoisin sauce
30 ml (2 tbsp) light soy sauce
15 ml (1 tbsp) chilli sauce

TO GARNISH
shredded spring onion
sesame seeds

1 Cut the chicken into very thin strips. Cut the red pepper, spring onions and carrots into similar-sized strips.
2 Bring a large pan of water to the boil. Add the noodles and cook for 2-3 minutes or according to the packet instructions. Drain thoroughly and toss with a little of the oil to prevent them sticking together; set aside.
3 Heat the remaining oil in a wok or a large frying pan. Add the chicken, ginger and garlic and cook over a very high heat until the chicken is browned on the outside and cooked right through.
4 Add all the vegetables to the wok or pan and stir-fry over a high heat for a

few minutes or until they are just cooked, but still crunchy.

5 Add the hoisin sauce, soy sauce and chilli sauce and stir to mix. Add the noodles and cook for a couple of minutes to heat through. Serve immediately, sprinkled with shredded spring onion and a few sesame seeds.

VARIATION
Replace the chicken with thinly sliced turkey escalopes. Increase the heat of the dish by frying a chopped chilli with the onion and ginger.

Pasta with Chicken Livers, Peas and Pancetta

Serves 4-6
Preparation 15 minutes
Cooking About 20 minutes
690-460 calories per serving

Smooth, rich chicken livers in a creamy wine sauce are perfectly balanced by the simplicity of plain cooked pasta in this tasty recipe. Peas lend a fresh sweetness, and a sprinkling of crisply cooked pancetta or bacon strips gives a contrasting crunchy texture.

50 g (2 oz) smoked pancetta, in one piece, or smoked streaky bacon, derinded and cut into strips

40 g (1½ oz) butter

3 shallots or 1 small onion, peeled and chopped

1 garlic clove, peeled and crushed

450 g (1 lb) chicken livers, trimmed and roughly chopped

30 ml (2 tbsp) finely chopped fresh parsley

120 ml (4 fl oz) dry white wine

50 g (2 oz) frozen petit pois or peas, thawed

400 g (14 oz) tagliatelle, preferably fresh plain or garlic and herb pasta

120 ml (4 fl oz) fromage frais (*not* low-fat)

salt and pepper

1 Cook the pancetta or bacon, without extra fat, in a small pan over a medium heat for 4-5 minutes until lightly browned and just crisp. Transfer to a plate; set aside.

2 Melt 25 g (1 oz) of the butter in a large frying pan. Add the shallots or onion and garlic and cook over a medium heat, stirring frequently, for 5 minutes until softened, but not brown.

3 Increase the heat and add the chicken livers to the pan. Cook, stirring frequently, for 4-5 minutes until browned and sealed. Stir in the parsley and wine and continue cooking over a high heat for 3 minutes or until about two thirds of the liquid has evaporated, leaving a rich sauce. Stir in the peas.

4 Meanwhile, add the tagliatelle to a large pan of boiling salted water and cook until *al dente*.

5 Drain the pasta thoroughly and return to the pan with the remaining butter. Toss to mix.

6 Add three quarters of the fromage frais to the chicken livers and cook, stirring, for 2-3 minutes over a medium heat. Remove from the heat and season with salt and pepper.

7 Serve the pasta topped with the chicken liver mixture. Add a spoonful of fromage frais to each serving and sprinkle with the reserved pancetta or bacon.

Chilli-fried Chicken with Coconut Noodles

Serves 6
Preparation 15 minutes
Cooking 10 minutes
540 calories per serving

Illustrated opposite

This spicy oriental noodle dish is ideal for a midweek supper dish as it can be assembled from storecupboard ingredients in a matter of minutes.

30 ml (2 tbsp) flour
5 ml (1 tsp) mild chilli powder
5 ml (1 tsp) ground ginger
2.5 ml (½ tsp) salt
5 ml (1 tsp) caster sugar
6 skinless chicken breast fillets, each about 150 g (5 oz)
250 g (9 oz) thread egg noodles
45 ml (3 tbsp) peanut or corn oil

1 large bunch spring onions, trimmed and sliced
7.5 ml (1½ tsp) Thai red curry paste or tandoori paste
150 g (5 oz) salted roasted peanuts, finely chopped
90 ml (6 tbsp) coconut milk
coriander sprigs, to garnish

1 Mix the flour, chilli powder, ground ginger, salt and sugar together in a bowl. Cut each chicken fillet diagonally into three pieces. Dip into the spiced flour and toss to coat well.

2 Cook the noodles according to the packet instructions; drain thoroughly.

3 Meanwhile heat the oil in a frying pan, add the chicken and fry for 5 minutes, or until cooked through; transfer to a warmed plate. Fry the spring onions in the oil remaining in the pan for 1 minute; remove and add to the chicken.

4 Add the curry paste to the frying pan with two thirds of the peanuts and fry for 1 minute. Add the noodles and fry for 1 minute. Stir in the coconut milk and toss the noodles over a high heat for 30 seconds.

5 Serve the coconut noodles topped with the chicken and spring onions. Sprinkle with the remaining peanuts and garnish with coriander.

Pappardelle with Rabbit Sauce

Serves 4
Preparation 15 minutes
Cooking About 1 hour
1080 calories per serving

This robust dish is based on a traditional Tuscan recipe from the heart of Italy. It makes an original and delicious alternative to the more familiar bolognaise sauce. If fresh rabbit is unobtainable, you can use 500 g (1-1¼ lb) frozen boneless rabbit.

900 g (2 lb) rabbit, cut into portions (see note)
125 ml (4 fl oz) olive oil
250 ml (8 fl oz) red wine
2 carrots, peeled and chopped
1 onion, peeled and chopped
1 celery stick, chopped
1 garlic clove, peeled and crushed
3 sage leaves

15 ml (1 tbsp) finely chopped fresh rosemary
225 g (8 oz) rindless streaky bacon, finely chopped
30 ml (2 tbsp) tomato purée
500 ml (16 fl oz) chicken stock
salt and pepper
400 g (14 oz) dried pappardelle

1 Rinse the rabbit under cold water, drain and pat dry on kitchen paper. Heat the oil in a large heavy-based frying pan (which has a lid). Add the rabbit and brown on all sides. (Do this in batches if necessary.) Remove from the pan and set aside.

2 Add the wine to the pan and cook over a high heat for 10 minutes. Add the carrots, onion, celery, garlic, herbs and bacon. Cook, stirring, for 15 minutes. Add the tomato purée and half of the stock. Return the rabbit to the pan and season with salt and pepper to taste. Cover and cook for 25 minutes, then add the remaining stock. Cook, uncovered, for a further 20 minutes, or until the rabbit is tender.

3 Lift the rabbit out of the pan; take the meat from the bones, shredding it as you do so. Return the meat to the sauce, check the seasoning, and cook for a further 5 minutes.

4 Meanwhile, add the pasta to a large pan of boiling salted water and cook for 10 minutes or until *al dente*.

5 Drain the pasta and toss with the rabbit sauce. Serve immediately.

Pasta, Veal and Rosemary Gratin

Serves 6
Preparation 30 minutes
Cooking About 2 hours
520 calories per serving

For this tasty gratin, you need the large pasta shells – *conchiglioni* – which are suitable for stuffing. If unobtainable use cannelloni tubes instead. Should you prefer to omit the veal from the recipe, simply double the quantity of minced beef.

30 ml (2 tbsp) olive oil
1 large onion, peeled and finely chopped
1 large carrot, peeled and finely chopped
3 celery sticks, finely chopped
1 large red pepper, cored, seeded and finely chopped
225 g (8 oz) minced beef
225 g (8 oz) minced veal
40 g (1½ oz) plain flour
300 ml (½ pint) beef stock
150 ml (¼ pint) red wine
30 ml (2 tbsp) chopped rosemary
1 bay leaf
salt and pepper
125 g (4 oz) Parma ham, finely chopped (optional)
150 g (5 oz) conchiglioni (large dried pasta shells) or 16 cannelloni tubes
50 g (2 oz) butter or margarine
600 ml (1 pint) milk
50 g (2 oz) pecorino or Parmesan cheese, grated

1 Heat the oil in a large sauté pan, add the onion, carrot, celery and red pepper and cook until the vegetables soften and begin to colour.
2 Add the beef and veal and cook over a high heat, stirring frequently, until it begins to brown. Stir in 5 ml (1 tsp) flour and cook for a further minute. Add the stock, wine, herbs and seasoning. Slowly bring to the boil, cover and simmer gently for about 1 hour. (If necessary, uncover towards the end of the cooking time to reduce the liquid to a thick sauce.) Stir in the Parma ham if using.
3 Preheat the oven to 180°C (350°F) Mark 4. Cook the pasta in a large pan of boiling salted water for 12-15 minutes until *al dente*. Drain well and cool slightly.
4 Fill the pasta shells or cannelloni tubes with the veal mixture and place in a single layer in a 2.4 litre (4 pint) ovenproof dish.
5 Melt the butter in a saucepan. Add the rest of the flour and cook, stirring, for 1-2 minutes before gradually adding the milk. Bring to the boil, then simmer, stirring, for 2-3 minutes. Remove from heat and beat in half the cheese, adding pepper to taste. Spoon over the pasta and sprinkle with the remaining cheese.
6 Bake in the oven for about 40 minutes or until golden brown and bubbling. Serve immediately.

'Everyday' Lasagne

Serves 4-6
Preparation 15 minutes, plus sauces
Cooking 45 minutes
465-310 calories per serving

This lasagne is ideal for a family midweek supper and it can be assembled relatively quickly if you keep a stock of bolognese sauce in the freezer.

1 quantity Bolognese Sauce (see page 19)
about 350 g (12 oz) fresh lasagne, or 225 g (8 oz) dried 'no need to pre-cook' (12-15 sheets)
1 quantity white sauce (see page 85)
45 ml (3 tbsp) freshly grated Parmesan cheese

1 Preheat the oven to 180°C (350°F) Mark 4. Spoon one third of the bolognese sauce over the base of a greased 2.3 litre (4 pint) ovenproof dish. Cover with a layer of lasagne, then spread over enough white sauce to cover the pasta. Repeat these layers twice more, finishing with a layer of white sauce to cover the lasagne completely.
2 Sprinkle the Parmesan cheese over the top and stand the dish on a baking sheet. Bake in the oven for about 45 minutes or until well browned and bubbling. Leave to stand for about 5 minutes before cutting.

NOTE: If using oven-ready dried lasagne, add a little extra stock or water to the sauce. Use a large rectangular or square ovenproof dish.

Classic Italian Lasagne

Serves 6
Preparation 20 minutes
Cooking About 2 hours
745 calories per serving

Many regions of Italy have their own lasagne recipe and this one comes from the Marche region which borders Tuscany.

350 g (12 oz) fresh egg lasagne or 225 g (8 oz) dried 'no need to pre-cook' lasagne (about 12 sheets)

MEAT SAUCE
10 g (⅓ oz) dried porcini mushrooms
15 ml (1 tbsp) olive oil
275 g (10 oz) onion, peeled and finely chopped
75 g (3 oz) carrot, peeled and finely chopped
75 g (3 oz) celery, finely chopped
125 g (4 oz) brown-cap or large button mushrooms, chopped
2 garlic cloves, peeled and crushed
450 g (1 lb) minced beef
125 g (4 oz) rindless streaky bacon, chopped
300 ml (½ pint) dry white wine

300 ml (½ pint) stock
15 ml (1 tbsp) tomato purée
10 ml (2 tsp) dried oregano
125 g (4 oz) chicken livers, trimmed and chopped
90 ml (6 tbsp) double cream
30 ml (2 tbsp) chopped fresh parsley
salt and pepper

WHITE SAUCE
50 g (2 oz) butter
40 g (1½ oz) flour
750 ml (1¼ pints) milk
60 ml (4 tbsp) double cream

TO FINISH
50-75 g (2-3 oz) Parmesan cheese, freshly grated

1 To prepare the meat sauce, put the dried porcini mushrooms in a bowl, pour on 100 ml (3½ fl oz) water and leave to soak for about 30 minutes.

2 Heat the oil in a frying pan. Add the onion, carrot and celery and fry gently for 5 minutes, or until softened. Add the fresh mushrooms and garlic; fry for 1 minute.

3 Stir in the beef and bacon; cook, stirring, over a high heat until browned. Stir in the wine, stock, tomato purée and oregano. Bring to the boil, cover and simmer for 45 minutes.

4 Meanwhile make the white sauce. Melt the butter in a large saucepan, add the flour and cook, stirring, for 1 minute. Off the heat, gradually whisk in the milk. Return to the heat. Bring to the boil, stirring, and simmer for 3-4 minutes or until thickened. Season with salt and pepper to taste. Stir in the cream. Set aside.

5 Preheat the oven to 190°C (375°F) Mark 5. Uncover the meat mixture, stir in the dried mushrooms with their liquor and the chicken livers. Simmer for 7-10 minutes, until the livers are cooked and the liquid is reduced by half. Add the cream and parsley and allow to bubble for 1 minute. Check the seasoning.

6 Grease a 2.3 litre (4 pint) rectangular or square ovenproof dish with butter. Spread a thin layer of white sauce over the base of the dish, then layer the pasta, meat, white sauce and Parmesan in the dish to make 3 layers of each. Ensure that the top is well covered with white sauce and a generous sprinkling of Parmesan. Cook in the oven for 1 hour, covering the top loosely with foil after about 20 minutes when the top is browned and bubbling.

NOTE: If using 'no need to precook' lasagne, add a little extra stock to the meat sauce and a little extra milk to the white sauce.

To prepare ahead, make both sauces the day before; cover and refrigerate separately. Warm the sauces through before layering up with the pasta as in stage 6.

Cannelloni with Beef and Roasted Garlic

Serves 6
Preparation 30 minutes
Cooking About 1 hour
470 calories per serving

Illustrated opposite

Don't be put off by the large number of garlic cloves in this recipe. Roasted whole, garlic has a mild flavour with a delicious sweetness that goes perfectly with red meat. You can buy cannelloni tubes ready for cooking and stuffing or, as in this recipe, you can roll up lasagne sheets to encase the filling.

12 sheets of lasagne (approximately)

FILLING
20 unpeeled garlic cloves (from 2 garlic bulbs)
30 ml (2 tbsp) extra-virgin olive oil
15 g (½ oz) dried porcini mushrooms
5 shallots, peeled and finely chopped

700 g (1½ lb) lean minced beef
175 ml (6 fl oz) red wine
30 ml (2 tbsp) chopped fresh thyme
salt and pepper

TO FINISH
150 ml (¼ pint) single cream
30 ml (2 tbsp) sun-dried tomato paste
75 g (3 oz) provolone or gruyère cheese, finely grated

1 Preheat the oven to 180°C (350°F) Mark 4. To prepare the filling, put the unpeeled but separated garlic cloves in a small roasting tin with 15 ml (1 tbsp) of the oil. Toss to coat the garlic in the oil and bake in the oven for 25 minutes until soft. Leave to cool.

2 Meanwhile, put the dried mushrooms in a small bowl and cover with 150 ml (¼ pint) boiling water. Leave to soak for 20 minutes then drain, reserving the liquor. Rinse the mushrooms to remove any grit, then chop finely.

3 Heat the remaining 15 ml (1 tbsp) oil in a saucepan. Add the shallots and cook over a medium heat for 5 minutes until soft. Increase the heat and stir in the beef. Cook, stirring frequently to break up the meat, until it is browned. Add the wine, mushrooms with their soaking liquor, and the thyme. Cook over a medium heat for 15-20 minutes or until most of the liquid has evaporated; the mixture should be quite moist.

4 Remove the papery skins from the garlic, then mash lightly, using a fork, to give a rough paste. Stir into the beef mixture, season with salt and pepper and set aside.

5 Cook the lasagne sheets in a large saucepan of boiling salted water until *al dente*. Drain thoroughly in a colander, rinse with cold water and drain again.

6 Lay the lasagne sheets flat on a board or work surface. Spoon the beef mixture along one long edge and roll up to enclose the filling. Cut the tubes in half.

7 In a small bowl, mix together the cream and sun-dried tomato paste. Season with pepper. Set the oven temperature at 200°C (400°F) Mark 6.

8 Arrange a layer of cannelloni in the base of a buttered shallow baking dish. Spoon over half of the tomato cream and sprinkle with half of the cheese. Arrange the remaining cannelloni on top and cover with the remaining tomato cream and cheese.

9 Cover dish with foil and bake in the oven for 10 minutes, then uncover and bake for a further 5-10 minutes until lightly browned and hot. Serve at once.

NOTE: The meat sauce may be prepared in advance and frozen if required at the end of stage 4.

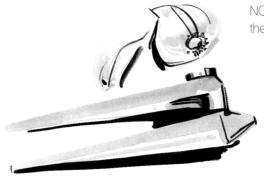

Spaghetti with Lamb Ragu

Serves 4-6
Preparation 25 minutes
Cooking 2½-3 hours
740-495 calories per serving

A good ragu needs long, slow cooking – for the sauce to reduce to a flavoursome concentrate and the meat to become meltingly tender. Tossed with perfectly cooked spaghetti and freshly grated Parmesan cheese this is real Italian comfort foot at its best.

45 ml (3 tbsp) extra-virgin olive oil
1 onion, peeled and finely chopped
2 garlic cloves, peeled and finely chopped
10 ml (2 tsp) fennel seeds, lightly crushed
2 carrots, peeled and finely diced
2 celery stalks, finely diced
350 g (12 oz) minced lamb
200 ml (7 fl oz) red wine
1 rosemary sprig
45 ml (3 tbsp) chopped fresh oregano
½ cinnamon stick
400 g (14 oz) can chopped tomatoes
salt and pepper
400 g (14 oz) dried spaghetti, fettucine or long fusilli
75 ml (5 tbsp) freshly grated Parmesan cheese

1 Heat the oil in a saucepan. Add the onion and garlic and cook over a medium heat for 5 minutes until softened but not browned. Add the fennel seeds and cook for 1 minute, then add the carrots and celery and cook, stirring, for 2 minutes.

2 Add the lamb to the pan and cook for about 7 minutes, breaking up the pieces with a wooden spoon, until browned. Increase the heat and stir in the wine. Let bubble for 4-5 minutes until the liquid has reduced by about half.

3 Add the rosemary sprig, oregano and cinnamon to the pan with the canned tomatoes and their juice. Bring to the boil and season lightly with salt and pepper. Cook, uncovered, on a very low heat for 2½ - 3 hours, stirring occasionally until the lamb is meltingly tender and the oil separates from the sauce. Remove and discard the cinnamon and rosemary. Spoon off the oil, soaking up any excess with kitchen paper. Adjust the seasoning to taste.

4 Just before serving, cook the spaghetti in a large pan of boiling salted water until *al dente*. Drain thoroughly.

5 To serve, toss the ragu with the pasta and about half of the grated Parmesan. Serve at once, sprinkled with the remaining Parmesan.

NOTE: The sauce tastes even better if it is prepared ahead, allowed to cool and left to stand for a while. Remove any fat from the surface and reheat thoroughly before serving. The sauce may also be frozen.

Braised Italian Lamb Shanks

Serves 6
Preparation 20 minutes
Cooking 3¾ hours
595 calories per serving

2 half leg knuckles of lamb
30 ml (2 tbsp) olive oil
30 ml (2 tbsp) dried porcini mushrooms, or 125 g (4 oz) fresh mushrooms
75 g (3 oz) butter
275 g (10 oz) onion, peeled and finely chopped
175 g (6 oz) carrot, peeled and finely chopped
175 g (6 oz) celery, finely chopped
9 sun-dried tomatoes, finely chopped
150 g (5 oz) Italian-style spicy sausage, thickly sliced
600 ml (1 pint) red wine
400 g (14 oz) carton or can of passata
600 ml (1 pint) vegetable stock
125 g (4 oz) dried pasta shapes
30-45 ml (2-3 tbsp) freshly grated Parmesan cheese

1 Preheat the oven to 240°C (475°F) Mark 9. Place the lamb in a large roasting tin and drizzle over 15 ml (1 tbsp) oil. Roast in the oven for 35 minutes.

2 If using dried porcini, soak in hot water to cover for 30 minutes, then drain. Finely chop the soaked or fresh mushrooms if using.

3 Meanwhile, melt the butter with the remaining oil in a large flameproof casserole. Stir in the onion, carrot and celery and cook, stirring, for 10-15 minutes or until soft and golden. Stir in the mushrooms and cook for a further 2-3 minutes.

4 Add the sun-dried tomatoes and sausage to the casserole with the wine, passata and stock. Bring to the boil, lower the heat and simmer for 10 minutes.

5 Lift the lamb from the roasting tin, place in the casserole and cover with a tight-fitting lid. Reduce the oven temperature to 170°C (325°F) Mark 3 and cook for a further 3 hours or until the lamb is falling off the bone.

6 Lift the lamb from the casserole to a deep, heatproof platter. Cover loosely with foil and keep warm in a low oven.

7 Stir the pasta into the casserole and return to the boil. Simmer for 10-15 minutes, or until the pasta is tender. Off the heat, stir in the grated Parmesan cheese and spoon around the lamb to serve.

Pastitsio

Serves 4
Preparation 10 minutes, plus cooling
Cooking 2 hours
675 calories per serving

This Greek-style lamb and pasta bake is flavoured with plenty of herbs and spices. Serve it with a leafy salad and a glass of robust red wine. For convenience, the meat sauce can be prepared ahead and frozen, at the end of stage 3.

45 ml (3 tbsp) olive oil
1 onion, peeled and finely chopped
2 garlic cloves, peeled and crushed
450 g (1 lb) lean minced lamb
7.5 ml (1½ tsp) dried oregano
5 ml (1 tsp) dried thyme
5 ml (1 tsp) ground cinnamon
5 ml (1 tsp) ground cumin
2.5 ml (½ tsp) ground ginger
2.5 ml (½ tsp) freshly grated nutmeg
1 bay leaf
400 g (14 oz) can chopped tomatoes

150 ml (¼ pint) dry white wine
salt and pepper
125 g (4 oz) dried pasta, such as penne or macaroni
45 ml (3 tbsp) chopped fresh coriander (optional)

CHEESE SAUCE
25 g (1 oz) butter
25 g (1 oz) plain white flour
450 ml (¾ pint) milk
50 g (2 oz) Parmesan cheese, freshly grated
2 eggs, beaten

1 Heat the oil in a saucepan, add the onion and garlic and cook gently for about 10 minutes, stirring occasionally, until the onions are soft.

2 Add the lamb. Cook over a high heat for about 5 minutes, stirring, until evenly browned. Stir in the herbs, spices and bay leaf. Cook over a moderate heat for a further 5 minutes, stirring occasionally.

3 Mix in the tomatoes, wine and seasoning. Bring to the boil, lower the heat and simmer, covered, for 30 minutes. Uncover and cook for about 15 minutes, stirring occasionally, until the sauce is thickened and well reduced. Adjust the seasoning. Cool and skim off all the fat. Discard the bay leaf.

4 Preheat the oven to 190°C (375°F) Mark 5. Cook the pasta in a large pan of boiling salted water until *al dente*. Drain and refresh under cold running water. Drain thoroughly, then add to the lamb with the chopped coriander, if using. Stir to mix, then spoon into a shallow ovenproof dish.

5 To make the sauce, melt the butter in a saucepan. Stir in the flour and cook, stirring, for 1 minute. Gradually whisk in the milk off the heat. Bring to the boil, stirring, and simmer for 3-4 minutes or until thickened. Cool slightly. Off the heat, beat in the Parmesan cheese and eggs. Pour over the lamb mixture.

6 Bake in the oven for 35-40 minutes or until golden brown and piping hot. Serve at once.

Pasta with Pork, Sage and Feta Cheese

Serves 4
Preparation 25 minutes
Cooking 20 minutes
890 calories per serving

Illustrated opposite

Slices of pork fillet stuffed with a herby feta cheese filling are served on buttered pasta ribbons with a cream and wine sauce.

450 g (1 lb) pork fillet
125 g (4 oz) feta cheese
30 ml (2 tbsp) chopped fresh sage or 2.5 ml (½ tsp) dried
60 ml (4 tbsp) chopped fresh parsley
salt and pepper
75 g (3 oz) butter

1 onion, peeled and sliced
150 ml (¼ pint) white wine
150 ml (¼ pint) chicken stock
150 ml (¼ pint) crème fraîche
350 g (12 oz) dried pappardelle or tagliatelle
sage sprigs, to garnish

1 Cut the pork into four equal pieces. Bat out between sheets of greaseproof paper until about 3 mm (⅛ inch) thick, using a rolling pin or meat mallet.

2 Blend the feta cheese with 15 ml (1 tbsp) sage and 30 ml (2 tbsp) parsley until smooth. Season with salt and pepper to taste.

3 Divide the cheese mixture between the pieces of pork and spread evenly. Roll up each piece and skewer with a cocktail stick.

4 Melt half of the butter in a heavy-based frying pan (with a lid). Add the onion and fry for 4-5 minutes. Add the pork and fry, turning, for 2-3 minutes until browned.

5 Pour in the wine and stock. Bring to the boil, then add the remaining herbs and crème fraîche. Cover and simmer for 10-15 minutes or until the pork is tender.

6 Meanwhile, cook the pasta in a large pan of boiling salted water until *al dente*. Drain thoroughly and toss with the remaining butter.

7 Remove the pork rolls from the sauce and cut into slices. Divide the pasta between warmed serving plates, top with the pork and pour over the sauce. Serve at once, garnished with sage.

Pasta with Chorizo

Serves 4-6
Preparation 10 minutes
Cooking About 50 minutes
950-630 calories per serving

Chorizo, the spicy Spanish sausage liberally flavoured with paprika, is available both raw by the piece, and cured ready to slice and eat. If you are unable to buy it raw in one piece, use cured chorizo – sold pre-packed in supermarkets – and cook in the sauce for 5 minutes only.

30 ml (2 tbsp) olive oil
1 onion, peeled and finely chopped
2 garlic cloves, peeled and crushed
30 ml (2 tbsp) tomato purée
30 ml (2 tbsp) mild paprika
1 dried chilli
2 bay leaves
2 fresh thyme sprigs
2 fresh rosemary sprigs

150 ml (¼ pint) dry red wine
425 g (15 oz) can chopped tomatoes
salt and pepper
450 g (1 lb) raw chorizo sausage, in one piece
400-450 g (14 oz-1 lb) fresh or dried pasta
chopped parsley, to garnish

1 Heat the oil in a heavy-based saucepan, add the onion and garlic and sauté for about 5 minutes or until softened. Add the tomato purée and paprika and cook for 2 minutes, stirring all the time.

2 Crumble in the chilli, then add the bay leaves, thyme and rosemary. Pour in the wine and bring to the boil. Cook for 2 minutes, stirring. Add the tomatoes with their juice and bring to the boil again. Lower the heat and simmer gently for 30 minutes. Season with salt and pepper to taste.

3 Cut the chorizo sausage into thick slices and add to the sauce. Cook for 15 minutes.

4 Meanwhile, cook the pasta in a large pan of boiling salted water until *al dente*. Drain thoroughly. Serve at once, topped with the sauce and sprinkled with plenty of chopped parsley.

Rigatoni Baked with Spicy Sausage

Serves 4-6
Preparation 15-20 minutes
Cooking 30-35 minutes
1000-670 calories per serving

You can use any good quality spicy sausages for this recipe, but – if at all possible – buy Italian-style uncooked sausages 'loose' from a good butcher or delicatessen, rather than prepacked ones. Prepare the sauce in advance if you wish, but don't toss with the pasta until ready for the oven, otherwise the pasta will become soggy.

45 ml (3 tbsp) extra-virgin olive oil

350 g (12 oz) uncooked spicy sausage

1 onion, peeled and chopped

2 garlic cloves, peeled and chopped

90 ml (3 fl oz) dry white wine

30 ml (2 tbsp) chopped fresh oregano

15 ml (1 tbsp) chopped fresh parsley

two 400 g (14 oz) cans plum tomatoes

5 sun-dried tomatoes, diced

12 black olives, pitted and sliced

salt and pepper

400 g (14 oz) dried rigatoni

175 g (6 oz) mozzarella cheese (preferably smoked), diced

50 g (2 oz) Parmesan cheese, finely pared

oregano sprigs, to garnish

1 Heat 15 ml (1 tbsp) of the oil in a large frying pan, then add the sausage, cut into lengths to fit the pan, if necessary. Fry on a medium high heat for 4-5 minutes, turning frequently, until lightly browned. Transfer to a plate and cut into slices. Set aside.

2 Add the remaining oil to the frying pan. Add the onion and garlic and cook over a medium heat for 5 minutes, until softened but not browned. Return the sliced sausage to the pan and add the wine and herbs. Increase the heat and cook for 3-4 minutes until about two thirds of the wine has evaporated.

3 Stir in the canned tomatoes and their juice, breaking them up with a wooden spoon. Add the sun-dried tomatoes and olives. Cook, uncovered, over a medium heat for 15-20 minutes until the tomatoes are pulp-like; do not reduce the sauce too much. Season with salt and pepper to taste.

4 Meanwhile, preheat the oven to 200°C (400°F) Mark 6. Cook the rigatoni in a large pan of boiling salted water until almost *al dente*, about 1 minute less than the cooking time. Drain thoroughly and toss with the sauce.

5 Turn into a greased large baking dish and scatter over the mozzarella and Parmesan. Bake near the top of the oven for about 15 minutes, until piping hot. Serve at once, garnished with oregano.

VARIATION
Use cooked sausages, such as chorizo, instead of raw ones. Omit stage 1. Simply slice the sausages and add at stage 2.

Cheese, Meat and Pasta Bake

Serves 6
Preparation 25 minutes
Cooking 35 minutes
745 calories per serving

75 g (3 oz) peppered salami, finely chopped

450 g (1 lb) minced beef

3 garlic cloves, peeled and crushed

30 ml (2 tbsp) chopped fresh parsley

50 g (2 oz) fresh white breadcrumbs

125 g (4 oz) Parmesan cheese, freshly grated

salt and pepper

1 egg, beaten

45 ml (3 tbsp) olive oil

250 g (9 oz) dried pasta shapes, such as penne or shells

1 kg (2¼ lb) passata

30 ml (2 tbsp) chopped fresh basil, parsley, thyme or chives, or 10 ml (2 tsp) dried mixed Italian herbs

400 g (14 oz) mozzarella cheese, diced

1 Combine the salami, minced beef, garlic, parsley, breadcrumbs and 50 g (2 oz) of the Parmesan cheese in a large bowl. Season liberally with salt and pepper. Add the egg and sufficient water to bind the mixture – about 100 ml

A delicious dish of mildly spiced meatballs tossed in a tomato sauce and baked with plenty of creamy mozzarella. Serve with a crisp green salad and crusty bread.

(3½ fl oz). Mix the ingredients together thoroughly with your hands, then shape the mixture into walnut-sized balls. Place on a tray and chill in the refrigerator for 30 minutes.

2 Preheat the oven to 200°C (400°F) Mark 6. Heat the oil in a non-stick frying pan and fry the meatballs in batches for about 5 minutes until golden brown and cooked through.

3 Cook the pasta in a large saucepan of boiling salted water until *al dente*. Drain well.

4 Mix the pasta with the passata, herbs and half of the mozzarella. Add the meatballs and seasoning to taste. Spoon into a greased 3.4 litre (6 pint) ovenproof dish. Sprinkle with the remaining mozzarella and Parmesan.

5 Bake in the oven for 30 minutes or until golden brown and bubbling.

NOTE: To prepare ahead, make up to the end of stage 4, a day in advance. Cover and chill in the refrigerator overnight. To use, continue from stage 5, allowing an extra 10 minutes cooking time.

Pasta Gratin with Mushrooms and Bacon

Serves 4
Preparation 20 minutes
Cooking About 30 minutes
760 calories per serving

Mushrooms, garlic and cream make an excellent effortless sauce for pasta. Smoked bacon adds a tasty bite to this recipe, but you could use canned or salted anchovies instead (see variation). Take care to only just cook the pasta, as the dish is then baked with a crispy crumb topping.

225 g (8 oz) dried rigatoni
salt and pepper
50 g (2 oz) butter
30 ml (2 tbsp) olive oil
1 large onion, peeled and sliced
1 leek, trimmed and thinly sliced
125 g (4 oz) smoked bacon, derinded and diced
4 garlic cloves, peeled and chopped

350 g (12 oz) chestnut mushrooms, sliced
30 ml (2 tbsp) roughly chopped fresh sage
200 ml (7 fl oz) crème fraîche

TOPPING
25 ml (5 tsp) black mustard seeds
40 g (1½ oz) breadcrumbs
15 g (½ oz) butter

1 Preheat the oven to 220°C (425°F) Mark 7. Cook the pasta in a large pan of boiling salted water until only just *al dente*; drain.

2 Meanwhile, melt half the butter with the oil in a large frying pan. Add the onion, leek, bacon and garlic and fry for 5 minutes until lightly coloured. Drain and toss with the pasta.

3 Melt the remaining butter in the pan. Add half the mushrooms with the sage and fry quickly for 2 minutes. Remove with a slotted spoon and set aside. Fry the rest of the mushrooms in the fat remaining in the pan.

4 Add the mushrooms to the pasta with the cream and seasoning. Toss the ingredients together until the crème fraîche has melted and coats the other ingredients. Turn into a flameproof gratin dish.

5 For the topping, heat the mustard seeds in a dry frying pan until they pop. Add the butter and breadcrumbs and stir over a low heat until the breadcrumbs are coated in the butter.

6 Spoon the breadcrumb mixture evenly over the pasta and bake for about 20 minutes until the topping is crisp and golden.

VARIATION
Replace the smoked bacon with 50 g (2 oz) can anchovies, drained, rinsed, dried and chopped.

Spaghetti with Spiced Meatballs in Tomato Sauce

Serves 4
Preparation 30 minutes
Cooking 20 minutes
965 calories per serving

Illustrated opposite

MEATBALLS
350 g (12 oz) shoulder of pork
175 g (6 oz) piece of gammon
175 g (6 oz) belly pork
2 garlic cloves, peeled
5 ml (1 tsp) coarse sea salt
5 ml (1 tsp) granulated sugar
15 ml (1 tbsp) coarsely crushed black pepper
5 ml (1 tsp) fennel seeds
1.25 ml (¼ tsp) dried chilli flakes

TO FINISH
30 ml (2 tbsp) oil
1 quantity fresh or rich tomato sauce (see page 17)
450 g (1 lb) spaghetti
oregano sprigs, to garnish
freshly grated Parmesan cheese, to serve

1 Trim the shoulder of pork, gammon and belly pork of any skin or connective tissue, then cut into rough chunks.
2 Place the meat in a food processor, add all the remaining ingredients and process until smooth. At this stage the sausagemeat is ready to use, but you can cover the bowl and leave it to mature in the fridge overnight if preferred.
3 With moist hands, roll the sausagemeat into small, even-sized balls.
4 Heat the oil in a frying pan and fry the meatballs in batches if necessary until evenly browned. Pour over the tomato sauce, bring to the boil and simmer for 10-15 minutes.
5 Meanwhile, cook the pasta in a large pan of boiling salted water until *al dente*. Drain and toss with the meatballs in tomato sauce. Serve garnished with oregano and topped with Parmesan cheese.

NOTE: The meatballs can be frozen in the tomato sauce at the end of stage 4. Defrost thoroughly before reheating to serve.

VARIATION
For a quicker version, replace the above meats with 450 g (1 lb) minced pork and 225 g (8 oz) unsmoked streaky bacon, finely chopped.

Spaghetti with Bacon and Walnuts

Serves 4
Preparation 10 minutes
Cooking 10 minutes
730 calories per serving

This tasty spaghetti dish is ideal for a fast supper. Vary the herbs as you like – try using oregano or basil instead of parsley.

350 g (12 oz) dried spaghetti
salt and pepper
50 ml (2 fl oz) olive oil
275 g (10 oz) rindless, unsmoked back bacon, roughly chopped
1 garlic clove, peeled and crushed
75 g (3 oz) walnut pieces, roughly chopped

450 g (1 lb) tomatoes, skinned (if preferred) and chopped
60 ml (4 tbsp) chopped flat-leaf parsley
grated rind of 1 lemon
225 g (8 oz) soft cheese, such as goats' cheese in olive oil

1 Cook the pasta in a large pan of boiling salted water until *al dente*.
2 Meanwhile, heat the oil in a large sauté pan, add the bacon, garlic and walnuts and sauté until golden, stirring occasionally. Stir in the tomatoes, parsley and lemon rind. Heat, stirring, for 1-2 minutes or until piping hot. Season with pepper to taste.
3 Drain the pasta thoroughly and toss with the bacon sauce. Serve each portion topped with pieces of soft cheese.

Pappardelle with Frazzled Prosciutto and Asparagus

Serves 4-6
Preparation 30 minutes
Cooking About 12 minutes
850-565 calories per serving

Illustrated on page 3

If you enjoy the distinctive flavour of prosciutto or Parma ham eaten raw as a simple starter or lunch with fresh melon, pears or figs, try including it in cooked dishes too. It's good on thin, crisp pizzas and – as in this recipe – water-thin slices are delicious 'frazzled' in a pan with olive oil. For a less substantial dish, omit the goat's cheese.

350 g (12 oz) frozen young broad beans, thawed
350 g (12 oz) asparagus, trimmed
90 ml (6 tbsp) extra-virgin olive oil
175 g (6 oz) prosciutto or Parma ham, in thin slices
3 shallots, peeled and finely chopped
2 garlic cloves, peeled and crushed
400 g (14 oz) dried pappardelle or other pasta ribbons
45 ml (3 tbsp) chopped fresh parsley
salt and pepper
300 g (10 oz) goat's cheese log, with rind

1 Slip the broad beans out of their waxy outer skins into a bowl and set aside.
2 Cook the asparagus in a pan of shallow boiling water for about 4 minutes until almost tender. Drain and refresh under cold running water; drain thoroughly. Cut into 5 cm (2 inch) lengths; set aside.
3 Heat the oil in a large frying pan. Add the prosciutto, in batches if necessary, and fry over a high heat for a few seconds. Lift out on to a plate; set aside.
4 Add the shallots and garlic to the frying pan and cook gently for 5 minutes to soften; do not allow to brown. Increase the heat to medium and add the broad beans. Cook, stirring, for 4 minutes.
5 Cook the pasta in a large pan of boiling salted water until *al dente*.
6 Meanwhile, preheat the grill to high. Add the asparagus to the frying pan with the parsley. Cook, stirring, for 2 minutes, then return the prosciutto to the pan. Season with salt and pepper. Remove from the heat.
7 Meanwhile, cut the goat's cheese into slices and arrange on a lightly greased baking sheet. Grill for 3-4 minutes until lightly browned.
8 Drain the pasta thoroughly. Gently reheat the prosciutto mixture if necessary, then lightly toss with the pasta in the large pan. Arrange on serving plates and top with the grilled goat's cheese. Serve at once.

VARIATION
Replace the broad beans with 75 g (3 oz) fresh rocket. Add to the pan with the asparagus and parsley.

Pumpkin and Prosciutto Ravioli with Butter and Herbs

Serves 4
Preparation About 45 minutes
Cooking 1¼ hours
490 calories per serving

Pumpkin makes a wonderful filling for pasta with its velvet texture, rich golden colour and distinctive nutty flavour. Here it is baked in the oven before mashing; boiling is a short cut to be avoided as it makes the pumpkin flesh too wet. Other firm-fleshed squash, such as butternut or acorn, can be used.

RAVIOLI
1 quantity pasta dough (see page 10)

FILLING
450 g (1 lb) wedge pumpkin
30 ml (2 tbsp) olive oil
75 g (3 oz) prosciutto or Parma ham, finely chopped
50 g (2 oz) provolone or Parmesan cheese, finely grated
20 ml (1½ tbsp) chopped fresh basil

20 ml (1½ tbsp) chopped fresh parsley
1 egg yolk
freshly grated nutmeg, to taste
30 ml (2 tbsp) double cream
salt and pepper

TO SERVE
25 g (1 oz) butter, melted
chopped fresh herbs, to taste

1 For the filling, preheat the oven to 190°C (375°F) Mark 5. Brush the pumpkin flesh with the oil and bake in the oven for about 1 hour until soft.
2 Meanwhile, make the pasta dough, wrap in cling film and leave to rest for 20 minutes.
3 Allow the cooked pumpkin to cool slightly, then scrape the flesh into a large bowl and mash until smooth. Add all the other filling ingredients and mix well.
4 If rolling out the pasta dough by hand, divide in half and roll into 2 sheets. If using a pasta machine, roll manageable portions into strips. Either way, roll out as thinly as possible. Keep covered with cling film to prevent them drying out.
5 Take a strip of pasta 10-12 cm (4-5 inches) wide. Spoon on heaped teaspoonfuls of stuffing at 6 cm (2½ inch) intervals. Brush the edges and between the stuffing with a little water. Cover with another sheet of pasta and press along the edges and between the stuffing to seal. Cut between the stuffing at 6 cm (2½ inch) intervals and cut neatly along the long edges. Repeat to use all of the pasta and stuffing, to make 20-24 ravioli.
6 Bring a large saucepan of salted water to the boil. Cook the ravioli in batches for about 3 minutes until the sealed edges are *al dente*. Drain thoroughly and transfer to a warmed serving dish. Add the butter, herbs, salt and pepper. Toss lightly to coat and serve at once.

NOTE: For step-by-step instructions on shaping ravioli, see page 13.
The ravioli may be frozen prior to cooking if required at the end of stage 5. Defrost thoroughly before cooking.

VARIATION
For a vegetarian version, replace the prosciutto in the filling with 50 g (2 oz) walnuts, finely chopped.

Tortelloni with a Tomato Butter Sauce

Serves 4
Preparation 30 minutes, plus pasta
Cooking 20-30 minutes
630 calories per serving

Illustrated opposite

Shaping these delightful tortelloni by hand is not a difficult task but it does require patience! Serve as a main course accompanied by a crisp salad.

1 quantity fresh pasta (see page 10)

STUFFING
175 g (6 oz) cooked ham, preferably smoked
125 g (4 oz) gruyère cheese, grated
25 g (1 oz) Parmesan cheese, freshly grated
30 ml (2 tbsp) chopped fresh parsley
1 egg yolk
salt and pepper

SAUCE
900 g (2 lb) ripe tomatoes, skinned, seeded and roughly chopped
1 large onion, peeled and quartered
2 garlic cloves, peeled and crushed
1 fresh oregano sprig
75 g (3 oz) butter
handful of freshly torn basil leaves

TO SERVE
chopped fennel or flat-leaf parsley
freshly grated Parmesan cheese

1 Wrap the pasta dough in cling film and leave to rest for 20 minutes.
2 Meanwhile, prepare the stuffing. Put the ham in a food processor or blender and process until finely minced. Add the remaining ingredients and process briefly until evenly mixed. Set aside.
3 To prepare the sauce, put the tomatoes in a saucepan with the onion, garlic, oregano and butter. Bring to the boil, lower the heat and simmer, uncovered, for 20-30 minutes until the sauce is thick and pulpy. Discard the onion and oregano. Season with salt and pepper to taste and stir in the basil.
4 Divide the pasta into 4 pieces; keep wrapped. Roll out thinly, 1 piece at a time, using a pasta machine if possible. Cut into 7.5 cm (3 inch) squares. To shape the tortelloni, place a teaspoon of stuffing in the centre of each square. Moisten the edges with a little water and fold each square diagonally in half over the filling to form a triangle. Press the edges to seal and bring the two corners together (see page 14). Repeat to use all of the filling and dough.
5 Bring a large pan of water to the boil. Add the tortelloni and cook for about 3 minutes until the sealed edges are *al dente*. Meanwhile reheat the tomato butter sauce. Drain the pasta and transfer to a warmed serving dish. Add the sauce, toss lightly and serve sprinkled with freshly grated Parmesan and chopped fennel or parsley.

NOTE: The tortelloni and sauce may be frozen separately at the end of stage 4. Defrost thoroughly then continue as above.

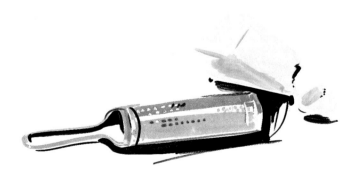

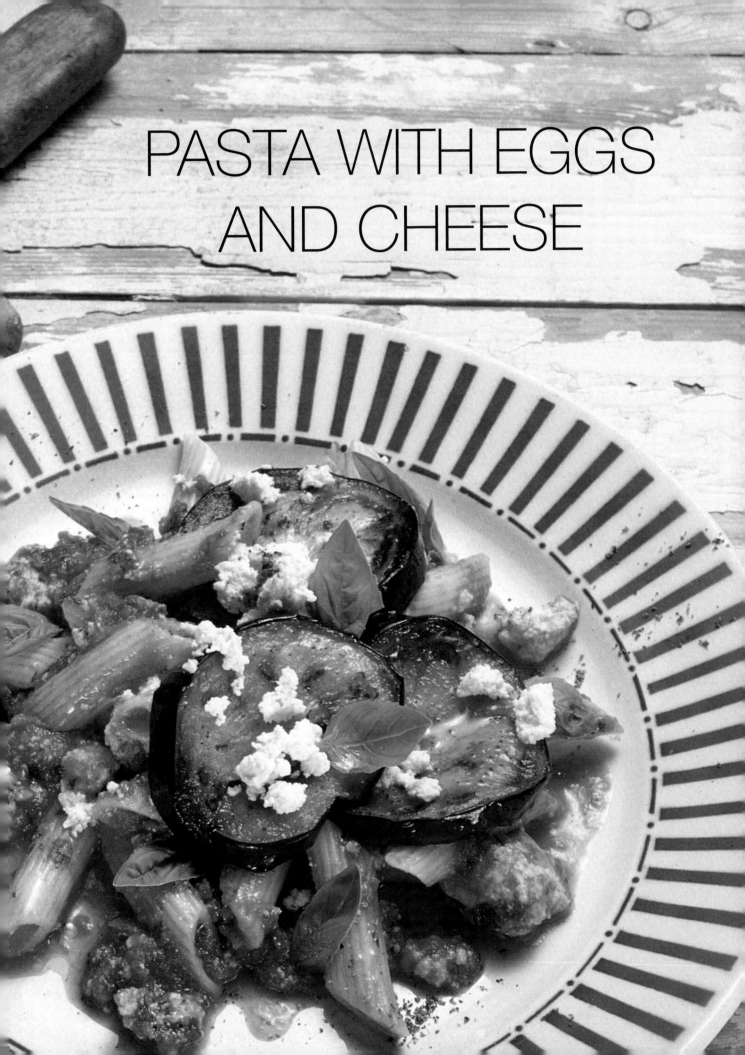

PASTA WITH EGGS AND CHEESE

Three Cheese Spaghettini with Celery

Serves 4
Preparation 20 minutes
Cooking 15 minutes
690 calories per serving

Illustrated opposite

A lovely, creamy dish combining three very different cheeses, served on a bed of celery and spaghettini. It's richly flavoured so serve small portions as a lunch or supper dish, accompanied simply by a glass of red wine and warm nutty bread, such as walnut or mixed grain.

150 g (5 oz) spaghettini
salt and pepper
50 g (2 oz) pine nuts
25 g (1 oz) butter
5 celery sticks, thinly sliced
150 ml (¼ pint) single cream
75 g (3 oz) mascarpone cheese
15 ml (1 tbsp) wholegrain mustard (optional)

30 ml (2 tbsp) white wine vinegar
45 ml (3 tbsp) extra-virgin olive oil
125 g (4 oz) blue cheese, such as Roquefort or Blue d'Auvergne, crumbled
100 g (3½ oz) goat's cheese log, sliced into 4 rounds
rocket or watercress leaves, to serve

1 Cook the pasta in a large pan of boiling salted water until *al dente*.
2 Meanwhile, toast the pine nuts in a frying pan until golden, then remove and set aside. Melt the butter in the pan, add the celery and fry gently for about 8 minutes until softened.
3 In the meantime, beat the cream with the mascarpone cheese, mustard, if using, seasoning and 15 ml (1 tbsp) wine vinegar until smooth.
4 Drain the pasta and toss with the olive oil, 15 ml (1 tbsp) wine vinegar and seasoning. Add the celery and pine nuts and toss to mix.
5 Preheat the grill to high. Season the slices of goat's cheese and grill for 3-4 minutes until golden. Turn the pasta mixture onto warmed serving plates and spoon over the cream sauce. Scatter with the blue cheese and slices of goat's cheese. Serve topped with plenty of rocket or watercress leaves.

Sicilian Aubergine and Ricotta Pasta

Serves 4-6
Preparation 15 minutes, plus standing
Cooking 35 minutes
870-580 calories per serving

Illustrated on page 101

Serve this delicious combination of creamy ricotta, tomato, aubergine, pasta and basil for lunch or supper.

2 medium thin aubergines
salt and pepper
450 g (1 lb) penne rigate or pasta shells
light olive oil, for shallow-frying

600 ml (1 pint) fresh or rich tomato sauce (see page 17)
225 g (8 oz) fresh ricotta, crumbled
50 g (2 oz) fresh basil leaves, shredded if large

1 Slice the aubergines thinly. Sprinkle with salt, place in a colander and leave to drain for 1 hour. Rinse well, drain and pat dry.
2 Cook the pasta in a large pan of boiling salted water until *al dente*.
3 Meanwhile, heat the oil in a deep frying pan. When hot, shallow-fry the aubergines in batches until golden. Drain well on kitchen paper. Reheat the tomato sauce.
4 Drain the pasta thoroughly, then add the tomato sauce, half of the ricotta and half of the basil. Toss well and transfer to a warmed serving bowl. Arrange the aubergine slices on top. Sprinkle over the remaining ricotta and basil and serve immediately.

Macaroni Cheese

Serves 4
Preparation 10 minutes
Cooking 35-40 minutes
780 calories per serving

225 g (8 oz) short-cut macaroni or small pasta shapes
salt and pepper
50 g (2½ oz) butter or margarine
65 g (2½ oz) plain flour
900 ml (1 ½ pints) milk

pinch of freshly grated nutmeg or 2.5 ml (½ tsp) mustard
225 g (8 oz) mature Cheddar cheese, grated
45 ml (3 tbsp) fresh wholemeal breadcrumbs

1 Cook the macaroni in a large pan of boiling salted water until *al dente*.

2 Meanwhile, melt the butter in a saucepan, stir in the flour and cook, stirring, for 1 minute. Remove from the heat and gradually stir in the milk. Bring to the boil and cook, stirring, until the sauce thickens. Remove from the heat. Season with salt and pepper, and add the nutmeg or mustard.

3 Drain the macaroni and add to the sauce, together with three quarters of the cheese. Mix well, then turn into an ovenproof dish.

4 Preheat the grill to high. Sprinkle the remaining cheese and the breadcrumbs over the macaroni cheese. Place under the grill until golden brown on top and bubbling. Serve immediately.

NOTE: To prepare ahead, make up to the end of stage 3. When required bake in a preheated oven at 200°C (400°F) Mark 6 for 25-30 minutes.

VARIATION
Divide ½ cauliflower into florets and cook in boiling salted water for about 10 minutes or until just tender; drain thoroughly. Mix with the cheese sauce and macaroni at stage 3. Finish as above.

Macaroni Cheese with Mozzarella and Fontina

Serves 4
Preparation 10 minutes
Cooking 20 minutes
770 calories per serving

Serve this luxurious version of an ever-popular pasta dish for a special occasion, accompanied by a tomato and basil salad.

225 g (8 oz) short-cut macaroni
salt and pepper
50 g (2 oz) butter or margarine
40 g (1½ oz) plain flour
900 ml (1½ pints) milk, preferably semi-skimmed
1 bay leaf
225 g (8 oz) Fontina cheese, grated (see note)

10 ml (2 tsp) Dijon mustard
large pinch of freshly grated nutmeg
125 g (4 oz) mozzarella cheese, chopped
50 g (2 oz) freshly grated Parmesan cheese
15 g (½ oz) fresh white breadcrumbs

1 Cook the macaroni in a large pan of boiling salted water until *al dente*.

2 Meanwhile, melt the butter in a saucepan, stir in the flour and cook, stirring, for 1-2 minutes. Gradually stir in the milk and add the bay leaf. Bring to the boil, stirring, and cook, stirring, until slightly thickened. Discard the bay leaf.

3 Off the heat, beat in the Fontina and mustard. Season with a little salt, pepper and nutmeg. Fold in the cooked macaroni, mozzarella and half of the Parmesan. Stir over a gentle heat until piping hot.

4 Spoon into a lightly greased, shallow 1.75 litre (3 pint) flameproof dish. Sprinkle with the remaining grated Parmesan and the breadcrumbs. Flash under a preheated hot grill to brown. Serve immediately.

NOTE: Fontina is a mild, buttery Italian cheese. If unobtainable, substitute Gouda or Edam.

Fettucine with Gorgonzola and Spinach

Serves 4-6
Preparation About 15 minutes
Cooking 2-10 minutes
630-420 calories per serving

The rich, creamy flavour of this pasta sauce belies its few simple ingredients. Serve accompanied by flavoured bread and, perhaps, a crisp colourful salad.

350 g (12 oz) young leaf spinach, trimmed
400 g (14 oz) fresh or dried fettucine, tagliatelle or long fusilli
salt and pepper

225 g (8 oz) gorgonzola cheese, diced
90 ml (3 fl oz) milk
25 g (1 oz) butter
freshly grated nutmeg, to taste

1 Place the spinach in a saucepan, with just the water clinging to the leaves after washing, and cook, stirring, over a medium high heat for 2-3 minutes until wilted. Drain well in a colander or sieve, pressing out any excess liquid.
2 Cook the pasta in a large pan of boiling salted water until *al dente*.
3 Meanwhile, place the gorgonzola in a clean pan with the milk and butter. Heat gently, stirring, until melted to a creamy sauce. Stir in the drained spinach. Season to taste with pepper; it shouldn't be necessary to add salt.
4 Drain the pasta thoroughly and add to the sauce. Toss well to mix. Serve at once, sprinkled with a little freshly grated nutmeg.

VARIATIONS
• For a milder alternative, use dolcelatte rather than gorgonzola cheese.
• Add 125 g (4 oz) diced cooked smoked ham to the sauce with the wilted spinach.

Cheesy Pasta Bake

Serves 4
Preparation 15 minutes
Cooking 45 minutes
550 calories per serving

Serve this rich, creamy bake with a tomato salad, or roasted tomatoes flavoured with garlic and herbs.

175 g (6 oz) dried pasta shapes, such as penne
salt and pepper
20 ml (4 tsp) olive oil
125 g (4 oz) onion, peeled and finely chopped

1 garlic clove, peeled and crushed
300 ml (½ pint) single cream
2 eggs
175 g (6 oz) Gruyère cheese, coarsely grated

1 Preheat the oven to 190°C (375°F) Mark 5. Cook the pasta in a large pan of boiling salted water until *al dente*.
2 Meanwhile heat 15 ml (1 tbsp) oil in a small frying pan. Add the onion and garlic and fry for a few minutes until beginning to soften.
3 In a large bowl, whisk together the cream and eggs. Season generously with salt and pepper.
4 Drain the pasta thoroughly and toss with the remaining 5 ml (1 tsp) oil. Combine with the onion and garlic, egg mixture and grated cheese.
5 Spoon into a 1.1 litre (2 pint) ovenproof dish. Stand the dish on a baking sheet and bake in the oven for 35-40 minutes or until the top is golden brown.

Beetroot Ravioli with Spinach and Ricotta Filling

Serves 4 (or 6 as a starter)
Preparation 40 minutes, plus pasta
Cooking 10 minutes
765-605 calories per serving

Illustrated opposite

These irresistible ravioli are prepared from vivid pink homemade beetroot pasta and filled with a creamy spinach and ricotta paste. The cooked ravioli are served with a simple, but delicious hazelnut and tarragon sauce.

175 g (6 oz) frozen leaf spinach, thawed
15 ml (1 tbsp) extra-virgin olive oil
1 small onion, peeled and chopped
1 garlic clove, peeled and crushed
finely grated rind of 1 lemon
175 g (6 oz) ricotta cheese
40 g (1½ oz) Parmesan cheese, freshly grated
1 egg yolk
salt and pepper

1 quantity fresh beetroot pasta dough (see page 11)
120 ml (4 fl oz) hazelnut oil
25 g (1 oz) hazelnuts, finely chopped
15-30 ml (1-2 tbsp) chopped fresh tarragon
tarragon sprigs, to garnish
freshly pared Parmesan cheese, to serve

1 Squeeze the spinach to remove all excess liquid, then place in a blender or food processor.

2 Heat the olive oil in a small frying pan, add the onion, garlic and lemon rind and fry for 5 minutes until softened. Remove from the heat and let cool slightly.

3 Add the onion mixture to the spinach and blend until fairly smooth. Add the ricotta, Parmesan, egg yolk and seasoning. Work briefly until evenly blended, then transfer to a bowl. Cover and chill for 30 minutes.

4 To shape the ravioli, roll out the beetroot pasta dough, using a pasta machine if possible, to form 8 pasta sheets (see page 12). Cut each one in half widthways. Lay one sheet on a well floured surface and place 5 heaped teaspoons of the spinach filling on the pasta at 2.5 cm (1 inch) intervals.

5 Using a wet pastry brush, dampen around the mounds of filling. Lay the second sheet of pasta on top and press around the mounds to seal well. Cut into squares with a knife or pasta wheel and place on a floured tea-towel. Repeat with the other pasta sheets to make 40 ravioli in total.

6 Bring a large pan of water to a rolling boil with 10 ml (2 tsp) sea salt added. Meanwhile, heat the hazelnut oil in a deep-frying pan. Add the nuts and fry for about 1 minute until turning golden. Remove from the heat.

7 Plunge the ravioli into the fast boiling water, return to the boil and cook for 3 minutes or until *al dente*.

8 Drain the pasta, reserving 60 ml (4 tbsp) cooking water and toss with the oil, nuts and tarragon. Add the reserved water, season with salt and pepper to taste and stir briefly. Serve at once, garnished with tarragon and topped with shavings of fresh Parmesan.

NOTE: These ravioli may be frozen. After cooking, refresh under cold water and pat dry. Toss with 30 ml (2 tbsp) olive oil and transfer to a large freezer bag. Seal and freeze for up to 1 month. Thaw at room temperature and cook in boiling water for 2 minutes before adding to the sauce.

VARIATION
To make large ravioli (as illustrated), don't halve the pasta sheets at stage 4. Position the filling at 5 cm (2 inch) intervals and cover with a second pasta sheet. Continue as above to make 20 ravioli.

Spinach and Ricotta Cannelloni

Serves 4-6
Preparation 30 minutes
Cooking About 1 hour
535-355 calories per serving

For this recipe cannelloni are shaped from sheets of lasagne rather than filling cannelloni tubes – which can be fiddly. If you cannot buy sheets of fresh lasagne use dried, but cook them first according to the packet instructions and reduce the final cooking time to about 20 minutes.

18 small sheets of fresh lasagne

SAUCE
30 ml (2 tbsp) olive oil
1 small onion, peeled and finely chopped
30 ml (2 tbsp) tomato purée
5 ml (1 tsp) mild paprika
two 400 g (14 oz) cans chopped tomatoes
pinch of dried oregano
300 ml (½ pint) dry red wine or vegetable stock
large pinch of sugar
salt and pepper

FILLING
30 ml (2 tbsp) olive oil
1 garlic clove, peeled and crushed
1 small onion, peeled and finely chopped
450 g (1 lb) frozen leaf spinach, thawed and drained
450 g (1 lb) ricotta cheese
freshly grated nutmeg

TOPPING
30-45 ml (2-3 tbsp) freshly grated Parmesan cheese or fresh breadcrumbs

1 Preheat the oven to 200°C (400°F) Mark 6. To make the sauce, heat the oil in a heavy-based saucepan, add the onion and fry for 5-10 minutes or until very soft. Add the tomato purée and paprika and fry for 2-3 minutes. Add the tomatoes, oregano, red wine or stock and sugar. Season with salt and pepper. Simmer for 20 minutes.

2 To make the filling, heat the oil in a large saucepan, add the garlic and onion and cook for 5 minutes, stirring all the time. Add the spinach and cook for 2 minutes. Allow to cool slightly, then add the ricotta cheese. Season with nutmeg, salt and pepper.

3 Lay the lasagne sheets on a work surface and divide the spinach mixture between them. Roll up the sheets to enclose the filling and arrange, seam-side down, in a single layer in a greased ovenproof dish.

4 Pour the sauce over the cannelloni and sprinkle with Parmesan cheese or breadcrumbs. Bake in the oven for about 30 minutes.

Spinach Tagliatelle with Blue Cheese and Spring Onions

Serves 4
Preparation 5 minutes
Cooking 2-10 minutes
695 calories per serving

400 g (14 oz) fresh or dried spinach tagliatelle
150 g (5 oz) ricotta cheese
150 g (5 oz) blue Stilton cheese
150 g (5 oz) crème fraîche

4-6 spring onions, finely chopped
15 ml (1 tbsp) chopped fresh coriander leaves
coarse sea salt and pepper
coriander sprigs, to garnish

1 Cook the tagliatelle in a large pan of boiling salted water until *al dente*.

2 Meanwhile, crumble the ricotta and Stilton cheeses together into a bowl. Add the crème fraîche and mix well.

3 Drain the pasta thoroughly and turn into a heated serving dish. Immediately add the crumbled cheese mixture, spring onions and chopped coriander. Using two forks, lift the tagliatelle to coat with the sauce. Season with salt and pepper to taste. Serve immediately, garnished with coriander.

VARIATION
Replace the spring onions with 225 g (8 oz) leeks. Clean the leeks thoroughly, then slice. Sauté in a little olive oil until softened. Add to the pasta with the crumbled cheese mixture and toss well.

Pine Nut Ravioli with Coriander Butter

Serves 4 (or 8 as a starter)
Preparation 40 minutes, plus pasta
Cooking 8 minutes
1170-870 calories per serving

Ground pine nuts, smoked bacon and Parmesan cheese make a delicious filling for these ravioli, which are served dripping in a tangy coriander butter. Serve as a special occasion starter, or main course with a leafy salad.

4 spring onions, trimmed and roughly chopped

75 g (3 oz) rindless smoked streaky bacon, roughly chopped

75 g (3 oz) pine nuts, toasted

pepper

30 ml (2 tbsp) olive oil

40 g (1½ oz) Parmesan cheese, freshly grated

1 quantity fresh pasta dough (see page 10)

beaten egg, for brushing

CORIANDER BUTTER

150 g (5 oz) lightly salted butter

45 ml (3 tbsp) roughly chopped coriander

30 ml (2 tbsp) roughly chopped parsley

5 ml (1 tsp) lemon juice, or to taste

TO SERVE

freshly pared Parmesan cheese

coriander or parsley, to garnish

1 Place the spring onions and bacon in a food processor and process until finely chopped. Add half of the pine nuts and some pepper and blend to a chunky paste.

2 Heat the oil in a frying pan, add the bacon mixture and fry for 3 minutes, breaking up the mixture with a wooden spoon. Stir in the Parmesan cheese and remaining pine nuts. Leave to cool.

3 If using a pasta machine, roll out a manageable portion of dough into strips. If rolling out by hand, roll out half of the pasta very thinly on a floured surface to a 50 x 30 cm (18 x 12 inch) rectangle. Repeat with the remaining pasta and cover with a clean damp tea-towel.

4 Place small teaspoonfuls of the filling in evenly spaced rows over one half of the dough, spacing them at 4 cm (1½ inch) intervals. Brush the spaces in between the filling with beaten egg. Lift the other sheet(s) of pasta over the top. Press down firmly between the mounds of filling and cut into squares, using a fluted pasta cutter. Transfer to a floured tea-towel and leave to rest for 1 hour.

5 For the sauce, place the butter, coriander, parsley and a little seasoning in a small pan. Heat gently until the butter melts, then add lemon juice to taste. Remove from the heat.

6 Bring a large pan of salted water to the boil, with a dash of oil added. Add the ravioli, bring to the boil and cook for 3 minutes, or until *al dente*.

7 Drain the pasta thoroughly, then transfer to warmed serving plates. Spoon over the butter sauce, scatter with Parmesan shavings and garnish with coriander. Serve at once.

VARIATION
For tortellini, cut the dough into 5 cm (2 inch) rounds. Spoon the filling into the centre and brush the edges with beaten egg. Fold the dough over the filling, then pull the ends together and pinch firmly to secure.

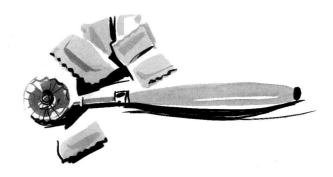

Deep-fried Rigatoni with Soy Dipping Sauce

Serves 4
Preparation 40-45 minutes
Cooking About 20 minutes
1015 calories per serving

Illustrated opposite

This unusual, delicious starter has an oriental influence. Tubes of pasta are stuffed with ricotta – flavoured with ginger, lime and coconut – and served with a soy and lime dipping sauce.

20-30 dried rigatoni tubes (depending on size)
salt and pepper

FILLING
250 g (9 oz) ricotta cheese
6 large spring onions, white part only, finely chopped
2.5 cm (1 inch) fresh root ginger, peeled and finely diced
125 g (4 oz) creamed coconut, grated
finely grated rind of 1 lime
½ plump red chilli, seeded and finely diced
30 ml (2 tbsp) chopped fresh coriander leaves
1 egg yolk

DIPPING SAUCE
15 ml (1 tbsp) sesame oil
30 ml (2 tbsp) soy sauce
30 ml (2 tbsp) red wine vinegar
juice of 1 lime
30 ml (2 tbsp) stem ginger syrup, or sugar to taste
½ plump red chilli, very finely diced

TO FINISH
plain white flour, for coating
1 egg white, beaten with 15 ml (1 tbsp) water
150-175 g (5-6 oz) day-old white breadcrumbs
oil or fat for deep-frying

TO SERVE
frisée (curly endive) or shredded lettuce
lime wedges
coriander sprigs

1 Mix all the ingredients for the filling together in a bowl and season with salt and pepper to taste. Cover and refrigerate until required.

2 Cook the rigatoni tubes in a large pan of boiling salted water for about 10 minutes or until just *al dente*. (If overcooked they may tear as they are filled.) Drain and refresh in cold water. Drain again and spread out on a clean tea-towel to dry.

3 To make the dipping sauce, mix all the ingredients together in a bowl and set aside to allow the flavours to blend.

4 Use a piping bag fitted with a large plain nozzle to fill the rigatoni. Spoon half of the filling into the bag. Pipe the mixture into the pasta tubes, blocking the bottom end with one finger as you do so; do not overfill. Repeat to fill the remaining rigatoni.

5 Toss the stuffed rigatoni in the flour, shaking off any excess. Dip into the egg white, then in the breadcrumbs to coat evenly, shaking off any excess. Place the rigatoni on a tray and refrigerate for about 20 minutes.

6 Divide the dipping sauce between 4 tiny serving bowls and set aside.

7 Heat a 7.5 cm (3 inch) depth of oil in a deep-fat fryer or deep saucepan to 160°C (325°F), or until a cube of stale bread sizzles as soon as it is dropped in. Deep-fry the rigatoni in batches, 5-6 at a time, for about 2 minutes until golden brown and crisp. Remove and drain on kitchen paper; keep warm in a low oven while cooking the remainder.

8 Arrange the deep-fried rigatoni on warmed serving plates with the frisée or lettuce. Garnish with coriander and lime wedges and serve at once with the dipping sauce.

NOTE: The rigatoni may be prepared up to the end of stage 5 and refrigerated overnight, or frozen for up to 1 month, then deep-fried from frozen.

Alternatively, the rigatoni can be prepared and deep-fried in advance, then reheated in the oven at 200°C (400°F) Mark 6 for 15 minutes.

Gratin of Spinach Ravioli with Porcini

25 g (1 oz) dried porcini mushrooms

15 ml (1 tbsp) extra-virgin olive oil

2 shallots, peeled and finely chopped

1 garlic clove, peeled and crushed

350 g (12 oz) ricotta cheese

2 egg yolks

100 g (3½ oz) freshly grated Parmesan cheese

salt and pepper

1 quantity fresh tomato sauce (see page 17)

1 quantity fresh spinach pasta dough (see page 11)

Serves 4 (or 6 as a starter)
Preparation 40 minutes, plus pasta and soaking
Cooking 12-15 minutes
800-535 calories per serving

For this variation on cannelloni, large pasta squares are topped with a rich porcini and ricotta mixture, then folded into triangles. These ravioli are cooked as usual, then grilled under a tomato and cheese sauce in individual gratin dishes. Serve as a starter, or with a side salad and bread as a main course.

1 Put the dried mushrooms in a small bowl, pour on 150 ml (¼ pint) boiling water and leave to soak for 20 minutes. Drain, reserving the liquid; finely chop the mushrooms.

2 Heat the oil in a small frying pan, add the shallots, garlic and mushrooms and fry for 5 minutes. Let cool slightly.

3 In a bowl, beat the ricotta with the egg yolks, 50 g (2 oz) of the Parmesan, the fried porcini mixture, and seasoning to taste.

4 Add the reserved mushroom soaking liquid to the tomato sauce. Purée in a blender or food processor until smooth, then transfer to a saucepan and heat through; keep warm.

5 Bring a large saucepan of water to the boil with 10 ml (2 tsp) sea salt added. In the meantime, divide the spinach pasta dough into 5 pieces. On a well floured surface roll one piece out thinly to a 25 cm (10 inch) square. Trim the sides and divide into 4 squares.

6 Place a heaped spoonful of the filling on one half of each square. Dampen the opposite edges with a little water, fold the dough over to form a triangle and press the edges together to seal well. Repeat with the remaining dough and filling to make 20 ravioli triangles.

7 Preheat the grill. Plunge the ravioli into the boiling water, return to the boil and cook for 3-4 minutes until just *al dente*. Drain well and pat dry. Transfer the ravioli to 4-6 individual gratin dishes.

8 Pour the tomato sauce over the triangles and scatter over the remaining Parmesan. Grill for 3-4 minutes until the cheese is melted and the sauce bubbling. Serve at once.

NOTE: To freeze, place the cooked triangles in a large gratin dish and pour over the tomato sauce. Cover and freeze for up to 1 month. Thaw at room temperature and bake, covered, for 20 minutes in a moderate oven. Transfer to the grill to brown the top.

Pasta with Caper Sauce and Grilled Cheese

Serves 4-6
Preparation 30 minutes
Cooking 15 minutes
755-505 calories per serving

Halloumi is a firm-textured Cypriot cheese with a salty flavour. It is wonderful for grilling or frying as it softens, rather than melts, and develops a lovely golden crust. Many supermarkets now sell halloumi, or it can be obtained from Cypriot food stores.

2 red peppers
90 ml (6 tbsp) extra-virgin olive oil
2 onions, peeled and chopped
2 garlic cloves, peeled and chopped
45 ml (3 tbsp) chopped fresh parsley

50 g (2 oz) capers in wine vinegar, rinsed and drained
salt and pepper
400 g (14 oz) dried penne, rigatoni or tagliatelle
225 g (8 oz) halloumi cheese

1 Preheat the grill to hot. Grill the whole peppers, turning occasionally until the skin is blistered and blackened all over. This will take about 20 minutes. Cool slightly then, over a bowl to catch the juices, peel away the charred skin and remove the seeds. Cut the flesh into strips and add to the bowl; set aside.

2 Meanwhile, heat 75 ml (5 tbsp) olive oil in a large frying pan. Add the onions and cook over a medium heat, stirring frequently, for 7-8 minutes until soft. Stir in the garlic and continue cooking for 2-3 minutes. Stir in the parsley.

3 Transfer the mixture to a food processor and add the capers and seasoning. Process briefly to chop coarsely.

4 Cook the pasta in a large pan of boiling salted water until *al dente*.

5 Meanwhile, cut the halloumi into 1 cm (½ inch) cubes. Place in a baking tin large enough to take them in one layer. Sprinkle with the remaining 15 ml (1 tbsp) olive oil and plenty of pepper; toss to coat the cheese. Grill, turning occasionally, for about 8 minutes until evenly golden on all sides.

6 Drain the pasta thoroughly and return to the pan. Add the caper sauce and reserved pepper strips. Toss to mix. Serve at once, topped with the grilled cheese cubes.

VARIATION
If halloumi is not available, use a firm goat's cheese log, cut into slices.

Pasta Cheese Omelette

Serves 2
Preparation 15 minutes
Cooking 10 minutes
780 calories per serving

This is an ideal way to use up left-over pasta, or cook some especially if necessary! Any type of pasta will do – long or short. Serve as a lunch or supper, with a mixed salad.

50 g (2 oz) butter
8 spring onions, trimmed and sliced
4 large eggs
50 g (2 oz) Parmesan cheese, freshly grated

salt and pepper
125 g (4 oz) cooked pasta, drained
1 mozzarella cheese, about 150 g (5 oz), cut into cubes
chopped parsley, to garnish

1 Melt the butter in a medium non-stick frying pan. Add the spring onions and cook for 2-3 minutes until soft.

2 Break the eggs into a bowl and whisk together with half of the Parmesan, a pinch of salt and plenty of pepper.

3 Add the pasta to the frying pan, stirring well to coat with butter. Pour over the eggs and cook gently until just beginning to set.

4 Scatter the mozzarella cubes over the not quite set omelette. Sprinkle with the remaining Parmesan and carefully fold the omelette. Cook for 2 minutes until the cheese is melted. Cut the omelette in two and serve sprinkled with chopped parsley.

VEGETARIAN PASTA

Spaghettini with Wild Mushrooms and Sage

Serves 4-6
Preparation 25 minutes, plus soaking
Cooking About 20 minutes
660-440 calories per serving

Illustrated on page 115

Not everyone is lucky enough to be able to buy – or find – wild mushrooms, but cultivated large field mushrooms work well in this dish too. Whichever combination of mushrooms you choose, the dried porcini will add a superb depth of flavour to the sauce.

15 g (½ oz) dried porcini mushrooms
575 g (1¼ lb) mixed fresh mushrooms, eg field, chestnut, oyster, plus chanterelles or other wild types, if available, cleaned
75 ml (5 tbsp) extra-virgin olive oil
3 shallots, peeled and chopped
2-3 garlic cloves, peeled and chopped

300 ml (½ pint) dry white wine
30 ml (2 tbsp) chopped fresh sage
30 ml (2 tbsp) chopped fresh parsley
salt and pepper
400 g (14 oz) dried spaghettini

TO SERVE
25-40 g (1-1½ oz) Parmesan cheese

1 To reconstitute the dried mushrooms, put them in a small bowl and pour on 125 ml (4 fl oz) boiling water. Leave to soak for 20 minutes then drain, reserving the soaking liquor. Rinse and chop the mushrooms.

2 Slice large field mushrooms; quarter chestnut mushrooms; leave oyster mushrooms and any others whole (unless very large).

3 Heat the olive oil in a large frying pan. Add the shallots and sauté over a medium heat for 5 minutes until softened. Stir in the garlic and cook for a further 1-2 minutes.

4 Add the chopped dried mushrooms to the frying pan with the soaking liquor and the wine. Bring to the boil, then lower the heat a little and allow to bubble for 8-10 minutes until the liquid has reduced by about half.

5 Add all the fresh mushrooms, except the oyster mushrooms, to the pan with the sage. Cook for about 6 minutes until they are tender. Stir in the oyster mushrooms, parsley and seasoning. Cook for a further 2 minutes.

6 Meanwhile, cook the spaghettini in a large pan of boiling salted water until *al dente*. Drain thoroughly and return to the pan.

7 Add the mushroom mixture to the pasta and toss lightly to mix. Adjust the seasoning and serve at once, sprinkled with shavings of Parmesan.

Calabrian Pasta

Serves 4-6
Preparation 10 minutes
Cooking 12-15 minutes
695-465 calories per serving

Illustrated opposite

The finest broccoli is grown in 'the toe' of Italy in Calabria – and called *calabrese* after the region. Fried with pine nuts, sultanas, garlic and breadcrumbs, it makes a delicious sauce to serve with pasta.

50 g (2 oz) sultanas
150 g (5 oz) broccoli
300-350 g (10-12 oz) ziti, long fusilli or spaghetti
salt and pepper
125 ml (4 fl oz) olive oil
75 g (3 oz) white breadcrumbs

2 garlic cloves, peeled and finely chopped
25 g (1 oz) pine nuts
15 ml (1 tbsp) sun-dried tomato paste (see note)
45 ml (3 tbsp) chopped fresh parsley
cayenne pepper, to taste

1 Put the sultanas in a bowl, pour on a little boiling water and leave to soak. Break the broccoli into small florets, cutting the stems into similar-sized pieces. Add the broccoli to a pan of boiling water, return to the boil and simmer for 30 seconds; drain.

2 Cook the pasta in a large pan of boiling salted water until *al dente*.

3 In the meantime, heat the oil in a frying pan, add the breadcrumbs and fry, stirring, until they begin to crisp. Add the garlic and pine nuts and continue to fry, stirring, until the pine nuts begin to colour. Add the broccoli and stir over the heat until it is thoroughly heated through.

4 Drain the pasta in a colander, setting it back on top of the saucepan to catch the last 15 ml (1 tbsp) cooking water. Stir the sun-dried tomato paste and drained sultanas into this liquid, then return the pasta to the pan. Toss with a

generous grinding of black pepper and half of the chopped parsley. Transfer to a heated serving bowl.

5 Mix the remaining parsley with the broccoli and crumb mixture. Add to the pasta and toss to mix. Sprinkle with cayenne pepper to serve.

VARIATION
For a non-vegetarian dish, replace the sun-dried tomato paste with 10ml (2 tsp) anchovy essence.

Pasta Primavera

Serves 4-6
Preparation 25 minutes
Cooking About 25 minutes
950-635 calories per serving

In this colourful dish, ribbon pasta perfectly offsets spring vegetables – or *primavera* as they are known in Italy. Some of the vegetables are cooked slowly until meltingly soft, sweet and buttery, while in contrast young asparagus, whole tiny carrots and sugar snap peas are cooked briefly to retain their fresh crispness.

175 g (6 oz) thin asparagus, halved

125 g (4 oz) sugar snap peas, topped and tailed

225 g (8 oz) carrots, preferably baby ones

50 g (2 oz) butter

1 small onion, peeled and chopped

1 red pepper, skinned, cored, seeded and diced

2 celery stalks, diced

6-8 spring onions, white part only, diced

2 courgettes, diced

400 g (14 oz) dried tagliatelle or pappardelle

salt and pepper

300 ml (½ pint) double cream

60 ml (4 tbsp) freshly grated Parmesan cheese

15 ml (1 tbsp) oil

20 ml (4 tsp) snipped chives

20 ml (4 tsp) chopped fresh chervil

20 ml (4 tsp) chopped fresh dill

1 Cook the asparagus in boiling salted water for 3-4 minutes, adding the sugar snaps after 2 minutes so that both are cooked until just tender. Drain, refresh with cold water and drain again; set aside.

2 If the carrots are tiny baby ones, leave whole; otherwise peel and cut into matchsticks.

3 Melt the butter in a large frying pan. Add the onion and sauté over a medium heat for 7-8 minutes until soft and golden. Add the red pepper and celery and cook for 5 minutes. Stir in the spring onions, carrots and courgettes and cook for 12-15 minutes, stirring frequently, until the vegetables are tender and beginning to colour.

4 Cook the pasta in a large pan of boiling salted water until *al dente*.

5 Meanwhile, stir the cream into the vegetables and bring to the boil. Allow to bubble, stirring frequently, for a few minutes until it is reduced by about one third. Stir in the asparagus and sugar snaps. Add the Parmesan and heat gently. Season with salt and pepper to taste.

6 Drain the pasta thoroughly and toss with the oil to prevent sticking. Pour the sauce over the pasta and sprinkle with the herbs. Toss well and serve at once.

VARIATIONS
Vary the vegetables according to availability. Fennel, broccoli florets, fresh peas and fine green beans are suitable options. Replace some of the herbs with 40g (1½ oz) chopped walnuts.

Pasta with Roasted Fennel and Peppers

Serves 4
Preparation 20 minutes
Cooking 20-25 minutes
490 calories per serving

Wide ribbon pasta always looks attractive served with vegetables. Here it is tossed in a light, creamy fresh-flavoured sauce and topped with roasted vegetables to make a sustaining supper.

1 fennel bulb, cut into 2.5 cm (1 inch) slices

2 yellow peppers, cored, seeded and cut into broad strips

1 red onion, peeled and sliced

2 garlic cloves, peeled

15 ml (1 tbsp) olive oil

150 ml (¼ pint) yogurt or crème fraîche

125 g (4 oz) ricotta or other curd cheese

30 ml (2 tbsp) milk

30 ml (2 tbsp) chopped fresh basil

30 ml (2 tbsp) chopped fresh parsley

salt and pepper

350 g (12 oz) fresh or dried pappardelle or tagliatelle

30 ml (2 tbsp) freshly grated Parmesan cheese

30 ml (2 tbsp) black olives

30 ml (2 tbsp) capers

flat-leaf parsley, to garnish

1 Preheat the oven to 220°C (425°F) Mark 7. Place the prepared vegetables and whole garlic cloves on a baking sheet. Brush lightly with the oil and bake in the oven for 20-25 minutes, until browning along the edges.

2 Meanwhile, place the yogurt, cheese and milk in a bowl. Add the basil and parsley, season liberally with black pepper and mix to form a pale green sauce. Transfer the sauce to a pan and heat through gently.

3 Cook the pasta in a large pan of boiling salted water until *al dente*.

4 Drain the pasta thoroughly, add to the sauce with the Parmesan and toss well. Add the olives and capers to the roasted vegetables. Serve the pasta topped with the roasted vegetables and garnished with parsley.

VARIATION
Omit the capers. Replace the fennel with 1 small aubergine, a few tomatoes and 1-2 courgettes; roast as above.

Olive Tagliatelle with Pesto Trapanese

Serves 4
Preparation 20 minutes, plus pasta
Cooking 2-3 minutes
565 calories per serving

This Sicilian pesto of garlic, basil, almonds, tomatoes and olive oil will complement any fresh or dried pasta, but it goes particularly well with homemade olive pasta.

1 quantity fresh plain or olive pasta (see page 10), or 350 g (12 oz) dried pasta

TO GARNISH
basil leaves

PESTO TRAPANESE
3 ripe tomatoes
4 garlic cloves, peeled
salt and pepper
50 g (2 oz) fresh basil leaves
125 g (4 oz) blanched almonds
150 ml (¼ pint) olive oil

1 To make the pesto, place all the ingredients in a food processor or blender and blend until smooth. Transfer to a bowl and set aside (see note).

2 If making your own pasta, allow to rest for 30 minutes, then roll out as thinly as possible, using a pasta machine if possible. Cut into tagliatelle and place on a floured tea-towel until ready to cook.

3 Bring a large pan of boiling salted water to the boil. Add the pasta and cook until *al dente*; fresh pasta will only take a few minutes. Drain well and toss with half of the pesto. Serve immediately, garnished with basil leaves.

NOTE: For this recipe, you will only need to use half of the pesto, but it isn't practical to make a smaller quantity. Spoon the rest into a jar, cover with a layer of olive oil, and seal. Store in the refrigerator for up to 1 week.

Pasta with Grilled Asparagus and Broad Beans

Serves 4
Preparation 20 minutes
Cooking 12-15 minutes
665 calories per serving

Illustrated opposite

Make the most of homegrown asparagus and fresh broad beans with this light, summery pasta dish. Accompany with a tomato salad and a glass of chilled white wine.

225 g (8 oz) shelled broad beans
salt and pepper
350 g (12 oz) dried penne or other pasta shapes
450 g (1 lb) asparagus, trimmed and halved crosswise
90 ml (6 tbsp) extra-virgin olive oil

2 garlic cloves, peeled and crushed
grated rind and juice of 1 lemon
45 ml (3 tbsp) chopped fresh mint
60 ml (4 tbsp) single cream
60 ml (4 tbsp) grated pecorino or Parmesan cheese

1 Blanch the broad beans in a large saucepan of lightly salted water for 2 minutes, then drain, reserving the water. Refresh the beans under cold running water and remove the tough outer skins.
2 Bring the reserved water to a rolling boil, add the pasta, return to the boil and cook for 10 minutes or until *al dente*.
3 Meanwhile preheat the grill. Place the asparagus on the grill rack, brush with a little oil and grill for 3-4 minutes on each side until charred and tender.
4 While the asparagus is cooking, heat 30 ml (2 tbsp) oil in a pan, add the garlic and lemon rind and fry gently for 3 minutes until golden. Add the beans, mint and cream and heat gently.
5 Drain the cooked pasta and immediately toss with the remaining oil. Add the asparagus and bean sauce, cheese and lemon juice. Toss to mix and season with salt and pepper to taste. Serve at once.

VARIATION
When in season, try using fresh peas in place of the broad beans.

Fresh Garlic and Basil Pappardelle with Tomato Sauce

Serves 4
Preparation 10 minutes, plus pasta
Cooking 45 minutes
450 calories per serving

A simple fresh-tasting tomato sauce is the perfect foil for this robustly flavoured pasta. Ready-made garlic and herb pasta is obtainable but the homemade version is far superior and very easy.

900 g (2 lb) vine-ripened tomatoes, roughly chopped
30 ml (2 tbsp) extra-virgin olive oil
2 garlic cloves, peeled and crushed
grated rind of 1 lemon
5 ml (1 tsp) dried oregano
30 ml (2 tbsp) chopped fresh basil

salt and pepper
pinch of sugar, or to taste (optional)
1 quantity fresh garlic and basil pappardelle (page 10) or 400 g (14 oz) ready-made herb tagliatelle
freshly grated Parmesan cheese, to serve

1 Put the tomatoes, olive oil, garlic, lemon rind and oregano in a saucepan. Bring to the boil, cover and simmer gently for 30 minutes.
2 Add the basil, salt and pepper to taste and a little sugar if required. Simmer, uncovered, for a further 20-30 minutes until the sauce is thickened. Keep warm.
3 Cook the pasta in a large saucepan of boiling salted water until *al dente*; freshly made pasta will only take 1-2 minutes.
4 Drain the pasta thoroughly and toss with the tomato sauce and some freshly grated Parmesan. Serve at once, with extra Parmesan.

NOTE: During the summer months when tomatoes are plentiful and at their best, make up several quantities of this tomato sauce and freeze for use during the winter.

Pasta Bows with Broad Beans and Asparagus in a Minted Butter Sauce

Serves 4 (or 6 as an accompaniment)
Preparation 30 minutes
Cooking About 10 minutes
585-390 calories per serving

Tossed with pasta in a fragrantly minted butter sauce, the delicate flavours of asparagus and broad beans marry perfectly. Serve this dish as a summer light main course, or as an accompaniment to poached salmon. Although skinning the beans takes extra time, the appearance of the dish is greatly enhanced and it is worth the effort.

25 g (1 oz) butter
6-8 spring onions (white part only), sliced
225 g (8 oz) cooked fresh or frozen broad beans
225 g (8 oz) dried pasta bows
salt
450 g (1 lb) asparagus, trimmed and cut into 2.5 cm (1 inch) lengths

TO GARNISH
mint sprigs

MINTED BUTTER SAUCE
1 large shallot, peeled and finely diced
45 ml (3 tbsp) white wine vinegar
150 g (5 oz) unsalted butter, cut into 12 cubes and chilled
salt and white pepper
lime juice, to taste
15-30 ml (1-2 tbsp) chopped fresh mint

1 Melt the butter in a frying pan over a low heat, add the spring onions, cover and cook gently for 10-12 minutes or until soft but not browned; keep warm.

2 Meanwhile, slip the broad beans out of their tough outer skins.

3 Cook the pasta in a large saucepan of boiling salted water until *al dente*.

4 In the meantime, add the chopped asparagus stems to a pan of boiling salted water and cook for 4-5 minutes, then add the tips and cook for a further 2-3 minutes or until *al dente*. Add the skinned broad beans to warm through. Drain and toss with the spring onions.

5 While the pasta and asparagus are cooking, make the butter sauce. Put the shallot, vinegar and 45 ml (3 tbsp) water in a small non-reactive saucepan. Reduce, by rapid boiling, until about 2 tablespoons of liquid remain. Over a very how heat add the butter, one cube at a time, whisking vigorously all the time, and making sure each piece is thoroughly incorporated before adding the next. Do not allow the sauce to get too hot otherwise it will curdle; take the pan on and off the heat as necessary. (This process shouldn't take too long.) Season with salt and pepper, and add a dash of lime juice to taste. Stir in enough mint to give a subtle flavour.

6 Drain the pasta thoroughly and toss with the vegetables and minted butter sauce. Serve immediately, garnished with mint.

NOTE: If you need to prepare the sauce a short while ahead, keep sauce warm by standing the saucepan in a large bowl of warm (not hot) water, stirring from time to time. Stir in the mint just before serving.

Tagliatelle with Artichoke and Olive Sauce

Serves 4
Preparation About 20 minutes
Cooking 10 minutes
620 calories per serving

Reserve this smart pasta dish for a special occasion. The olives are an important ingredient, so buy the best you can find.

250 g (9 oz) fresh or dried plain, herb or spinach tagliatelle
salt and pepper

SAUCE
30 ml (2 tbsp) olive oil
1 large garlic clove, peeled and crushed
two 425 g (15 oz) cans artichoke hearts, quartered

100-125 g (3½-4 oz) pitted green olives, chopped
250 g (9 oz) mascarpone cheese
grated rind of 1 lemon
pinch of sugar, to taste
60 ml (4 tbsp) chopped mixed fresh herbs, such as oregano, chives, thyme and parsley

1 If using dried pasta, cook in a large pan of boiling salted water until *al dente*.

2 Meanwhile, prepare the sauce. Heat the oil in a large, heavy-based sauté pan over a moderate heat. Add the garlic and fry for 1 minute until softened but not coloured. Add the artichokes and green olives, stir to coat with the oil, and cook for a further 2 minutes.

3 Meanwhile, mix the mascarpone with the lemon rind and 125 ml (4 fl oz) water. Pour into the pan and bring to the boil. Reduce the heat and simmer for 5 minutes. Add salt, pepper and sugar to taste. If using fresh pasta cook at this stage (as above) until *al dente*.

4 Drain the pasta thoroughly and turn into a warmed serving bowl. Stir two thirds of the herbs into the artichoke and green olive sauce, then pour over the pasta. Serve immediately, sprinkled with the rest of the herbs.

Spaghetti with Leeks, Peas and Saffron Cream

Serves 4-6
Preparation 10 minutes
Cooking 15 minutes
925-615 calories per serving

Saffron adds its distinctive golden colour and inimitable flavour to this creamy vegetable and pasta dish. Serve accompanied by a crisp salad – either green and leafy, or try lightly cooked baby carrots dressed in a little vinaigrette as a pretty option.

1.25 ml (¼ tsp) saffron threads
50 g (2 oz) butter
350 g (12 oz) trimmed leeks, thinly sliced
150 g (5 oz) frozen peas, thawed
400 g (14 oz) dried spaghetti or paglia e fieno

300 ml (½ pint) extra-thick double cream
90 ml (6 tbsp) freshly grated Parmesan cheese
salt and pepper
chervil or parsley sprigs, to garnish

1 Crumble the saffron into a small bowl, cover with 60 ml (4 tbsp) boiling water and leave to stand.

2 Melt the butter in a large frying pan. Add the leeks and cook over a medium heat, stirring, for 7-8 minutes to soften. Add the peas and continue cooking for a further 3 minutes.

3 Meanwhile, cook the pasta in plenty of boiling salted water until *al dente*.

4 Add the saffron liquid and the cream to the leeks and peas. Heat gently until simmering. Stir in half of the Parmesan and remove from the heat. Season with salt and pepper.

5 Drain the pasta thoroughly and return to the pan. Add the sauce and toss lightly to mix. Add the remaining Parmesan cheese and toss again. Serve at once, garnished with chervil or parsley.

VARIATION
For a non-vegetarian option, add 225 g (8 oz) cooked peeled prawns to the sauce at the end of stage 4 once the pasta is cooked. Reheat gently and continue as above.

Lemon Tagliatelle with Summer Vegetables and Herb Sauce

Serves 4-6
Preparation 20 minutes, plus pasta
Cooking 10 minutes
715-475 calories per serving

Illustrated opposite

This vibrant, refreshing dish is perfect for a summer supper with the added bonus that it is very quick and simple once you have made the pasta! (If very short of time you can, of course, use ordinary dried tagliatelle.) Vary the vegetables as you like, although this combination is well balanced and colourful.

25 g (1 oz) mixed fresh herbs, such as basil, chervil, chives, dill, parsley, roughly chopped
5 ml (1 tsp) dried oregano
120 ml (4 fl oz) extra-virgin olive oil
700 g (1½ lb) mixed summer vegetables to include: cherry tomatoes (optional), courgettes, asparagus tips, French beans, shelled broad beans and/or peas, baby carrots

2 shallots, peeled and finely chopped
1 garlic clove, peeled and crushed
90 ml (6 tbsp) single cream
1 quantity fresh lemon tagliatelle (see page 10), or 400 g (14 oz) dried tagliatelle
salt and pepper

TO SERVE
freshly pared Parmesan cheese

1 Place the fresh herbs and dried oregano in a bowl. Add all but 30 ml (2 tbsp) of the olive oil. Stir well and set aside for a few hours if possible, to infuse.
2 Prepare the vegetables. Thinly slice the courgettes; trim the asparagus spears; trim the French beans; peel the carrots and halve lengthwise if large.
3 Blanch all the vegetables, except the tomatoes, separately, in a large pan of lightly salted boiling water for 1-3 minutes depending on size and the vegetable (see note). Drain and immediately refresh under cold water. Pat dry.
4 Heat the remaining oil in a large frying pan, add the shallots and garlic and sauté for 5 minutes. Add the vegetables to the pan, stir-fry over a gentle heat and add the herb mixture.
5 Meanwhile cook the tagliatelle in a large pan of boiling salted water until *al dente*; fresh pasta will only take 1-2 minutes.
6 Drain the pasta, reserving 60 ml (4 tbsp) of the cooking water. Add the pasta and water to the frying pan and toss with the vegetables and herb sauce. Stir in the cream and heat through briefly. Serve at once, seasoned with salt and pepper, and scattered liberally with Parmesan shavings.

NOTE: The vegetables are listed in order of blanching time required: courgette slices take the shortest time; baby carrots the longest.

Spaghetti, Aubergine and Mozzarella

Serves 4
Preparation 10 minutes
Cooking 20 minutes
745 calories per serving

A quick and easy supper dish, flavoured with basil, pine nuts and creamy mozzarella.

90 ml (3 fl oz) olive oil
1 onion, peeled and chopped
2 garlic cloves, peeled and crushed
1 medium aubergine, about 400 g (14 oz), cut into small chunks
400 g (14 oz) can chopped tomatoes
salt and pepper
350 g (12 oz) dried spaghetti

30 ml (2 tbsp) capers in wine vinegar, drained
15 g (½ oz) fresh basil leaves, shredded
150 g (5 oz) mozzarella cheese, diced
30 ml (2 tbsp) pine nuts
60 ml (4 tbsp) freshly grated Parmesan cheese

1 Heat half the oil in a frying pan. Add the onion, garlic and aubergine, and sauté for 8-10 minutes. Add the tomatoes and seasoning. Bring to the boil lower the heat and simmer for 15 minutes.
2 Meanwhile, cook the pasta in plenty of boiling salted water until *al dente*.
3 Drain the pasta, return to the pan and toss with the tomato and aubergine mixture. Add the capers, basil, mozzarella and pine nuts; toss well. Check the seasoning, and serve at once, with the grated Parmesan handed separately.

Tagliatelle with Pumpkin and Blue Cheese Sauce

Serves 4-6
Preparation 15 minutes
Cooking About 12 minutes
930-620 calories per serving

This rich combination of pumpkin, cream and dolcelatte with broad pasta ribbons is best served with a simple salad and, perhaps, some good brown bread. Other firm-fleshed squashes, such as butternut or acorn squash, can be used with equally good results when pumpkin is out of season.

350 g (12 oz) wedge of pumpkin, peeled and seeded
25 g (1 oz) butter
1 garlic clove, peeled and crushed
30 ml (2 tbsp) chopped fresh parsley
300 ml (½ pint) extra-thick double cream
1.25 ml (¼ tsp) freshly grated nutmeg

400 g (14 oz) dried tagliatelle, pappardelle or fusilli
175 g (6 oz) dolcelatte cheese
salt and pepper

TO GARNISH
30 ml (2 tbsp) pine nuts, toasted
15 ml (1 tbsp) chopped fresh parsley

1 Grate the pumpkin flesh, using a food processor with a grating attachment, or by hand.
2 Melt the butter in a large frying pan. Add the pumpkin and garlic and cook, stirring, over a medium heat for about 5 minutes, until softened. Stir in the parsley, cream and nutmeg and cook for a further 2 minutes.
3 Cook the pasta in a large pan of boiling salted water until *al dente*.
4 Cut the dolcelatte into small pieces and add to the sauce. Heat gently, stirring until melted. Season with salt and pepper to taste.
5 Drain the pasta thoroughly and return to the pan. Add the pumpkin and cheese sauce, and toss well to mix. Serve at once, sprinkled with toasted pine nuts and chopped parsley.

VARIATION
Replace the dolcelatte with 175 g (6 oz) *Boursin* or other garlic and herb-flavoured cheese.

Penne with Spicy Squash Sauce

Serves 4-6
Preparation 25 minutes
Cooking About 1 hour
500-340 calories per serving

A highly flavoured sauce of chunky squash, aubergine, chick peas and carrots simmered in warm, spicy juices gives a wonderful, glossy coating to the pasta. Other types of squash or pumpkin can be used instead of the butternut.

1 butternut squash, about 700 g (1½ lb)
25 g (1 oz) butter
30 ml (2 tbsp) olive oil
225 g (8 oz) shallots or baby onions, peeled
1 cinnamon stick
2.5 cm (1 inch) piece fresh root ginger, peeled and grated
2.5 ml (½ tsp) ground turmeric
1 small aubergine, cut into 1 cm (½ inch) chunks
1 small red or green chilli, seeded and finely chopped

10 ml (2 tsp) plain flour
450 ml (¾ pint) vegetable stock
425 g (15 oz) can chick peas, rinsed and drained
25 g (1 oz) raisins
5 ml (1 tsp) dark muscovado sugar, or to taste
10 ml (2 tsp) lemon juice
175 g (6 oz) dried penne or other pasta shapes
salt and pepper
coriander leaves, to garnish

1 Pierce the skin of the squash and cook in boiling water for 30 minutes or until the flesh feels tender when pierced with a knife. Drain and leave until cool enough to handle, then halve and scoop out the seeds. Cut away the skin and roughly dice the flesh.
2 Melt the butter with the oil in a large pan. Add the shallots or onions, cinnamon, ginger and turmeric. Cook gently for 10 minutes, stirring. Add the aubergine and chilli and cook for a further 5 minutes.
3 Stir in the flour, then gradually stir in the stock. Add the chick peas, raisins,

sugar and lemon juice, and bring just to the boil. Cover and simmer gently for 10 minutes until the vegetables are tender.

4 Meanwhile, add the pasta to a large pan of boiling salted water and cook until *al dente*.

5 Drain the pasta and add to the sauce with the squash. Heat through for 1-2 minutes, tossing the ingredients lightly together. Season with salt and pepper to taste and serve scattered with coriander leaves.

NOTE: For convenience, the sauce can be made ahead, ready for tossing with the freshly cooked pasta.

Fried Courgette Ribbons with Linguine

Serves 4-6
Preparation 30 minutes
Cooking 20 minutes
850-565 calories per serving

Tender courgette ribbons in a crisp, golden Parmesan crust contrast with a creamy smooth tomato sauce in this unusual pasta dish. The courgette ribbons take a little time to prepare, so to compensate the sauce is very simple and can be made ahead if preferred.

400 g (14 oz) dried linguine

TOMATO SAUCE
45 ml (3 tbsp) olive oil
1 onion, peeled and roughly chopped
1 garlic clove, peeled and roughly chopped
400 g (14 oz) can chopped tomatoes
45 ml (3 tbsp) chopped fresh basil or oregano
salt and pepper
45 ml (3 tbsp) double cream

COURGETTE RIBBONS
350 g (12 oz) small courgettes
2 eggs
225 g (8 oz) dry white breadcrumbs
25 g (1 oz) freshly grated Parmesan cheese
10 ml (2 tsp) dried thyme
oil for deep-frying

TO FINISH
45 ml (3 tbsp) freshly grated Parmesan cheese
balsamic vinegar, to serve

1 To prepare the sauce, heat the oil in a saucepan, add the onion and garlic and cook over a medium heat, stirring frequently, for 5 minutes, to soften. Add the tomatoes and herbs and bring to the boil. Lower the heat and simmer for 10 minutes. Season with salt and pepper.

2 Purée the sauce in a blender or food processor, then sieve the mixture back into the pan. Stir in the cream; set aside.

3 Using a vegetable peeler and pressing firmly, pare the courgettes into long 'ribbons'. Lightly beat the eggs in a shallow bowl. In a separate shallow bowl mix the breadcrumbs with the Parmesan, thyme, salt and pepper.

4 Heat the oil for deep-frying. Dip the courgette ribbons, one at a time, first into the beaten egg and then into the breadcrumb mixture to coat.

5 Cook the pasta in a large pan of boiling salted water until *al dente*.

6 Meanwhile, fry the courgette ribbons, in batches, in the hot oil for 1-2 minutes, until golden and crisp. Drain on kitchen paper then transfer to a plate and keep hot.

7 Gently reheat the tomato sauce. Drain the pasta thoroughly, then return to the pan. Add the sauce and Parmesan and toss lightly. Pile onto warmed serving plates and top with the courgette ribbons. Serve at once, accompanied by balsamic vinegar for sprinkling.

NOTE: If you do not have any balsamic vinegar, serve with lemon wedges instead. To add colour, snip a few chives over the pasta before topping with the fried courgette ribbons.

Lasagnette with Courgettes and Sun-dried Tomatoes

Serves 4
Preparation 25 minutes
Cooking About 10 minutes
625 calories per serving

Illustrated opposite

For this pretty pasta dish, the piquant tomato sauce is served separately, at room temperature. Any flat wide pasta would be a suitable alternative for the lasagnette. Use purple basil if you have some to hand. Serve as a vegetarian main course, with warm foccacia or flavoured bread.

250 g (9 oz) dried lasagnette
8 small, thin courgettes
salt and pepper
15 ml (1 tbsp) olive oil
8 sun-dried tomatoes in oil, cut into wide strips
finely pared rind of 1 lemon, shredded
6 large basil leaves, shredded

SAUCE
1 tomato, quartered
50 g (2 oz) sun-dried tomatoes in oil, drained and roughly chopped
2 garlic cloves, peeled and chopped

50 g (2 oz) pine nuts
50 g (2 oz) Parmesan cheese, freshly grated
30 ml (2 tbsp) olive oil
30 ml (2 tbsp) oil from the sun-dried tomato jar
juice of 1 lemon
10 ml (2 tsp) grated horseradish (optional)
5-10 ml (1-2 tsp) soft brown sugar, to taste

TO GARNISH
basil sprigs

1 Break the lasagnette strips in half. Pare the courgettes into long thin ribbons, using a swivel vegetable peeler or mandolin.
2 To make the sauce, put the fresh tomato, sun-dried tomatoes and garlic in a blender or food processor and work to a purée. Add the remaining ingredients together with 30 ml (2 tbsp) warm water and work until evenly blended. Season to taste and add a little more sugar if required. If the sauce is too thick, thin with a little more water. Transfer to a serving bowl.
3 Cook the lasagnette in a large saucepan of boiling salted water until *al dente*.
4 Meanwhile, heat the oil in a frying pan and quickly stir-fry the courgette ribbons, in batches, for 2-3 minutes or until just *al dente*. Remove from the heat and add the sun-dried tomatoes and lemon rind.
5 Drain the pasta well and toss with the courgette mixture and shredded basil. Transfer to a warmed serving bowl and garnish with the basil leaves. Serve the sauce separately at room temperature.

Rigatoni with Artichokes in a Creamy Sauce

Serves 4
Preparation 10 minutes
Cooking 15 minutes
660 calories per serving

This simple, quick supper dish uses artichokes preserved in oil which are available from most supermarkets. It can be assembled in minutes.

150 g (5 oz) butter
75 g (3 oz) fresh white breadcrumbs
1 garlic clove, peeled and crushed
400 g (14 oz) dried rigatoni
salt and pepper

grated rind of 1 lemon
300 ml (½ pint) single cream
pinch of freshly grated nutmeg
250 g (9 oz) jar artichoke hearts preserved in oil, drained
30 ml (2 tbsp) chopped fresh parsley

1 Melt 50 g (2 oz) of the butter in a frying pan. Add the breadcrumbs and garlic, and fry until crisp and golden. Remove from the pan and set aside.
2 Cook the pasta in a large saucepan of boiling salted water until *al dente*.
3 Meanwhile, melt the remaining butter in a pan, add the lemon rind and cook gently for a few seconds. Add the cream and season with salt, pepper and nutmeg. Bring to the boil and cook until reduced and thickened.
4 Cut the artichokes into quarters and stir them into the cream sauce; keep warm.
5 Drain the pasta thoroughly and return to the saucepan. Add the lemon cream sauce, artichokes and chopped parsley; mix thoroughly. Serve at once, topped with the fried breadcrumbs.

Buckwheat Pasta with Grilled Radicchio

Serves 4
Preparation 20 minutes, plus pasta
Cooking 15 minutes
575 calories per serving

Illustrated opposite

Grilling mellows the bitter taste of radicchio and imparts a wonderful smoky flavour. Sweet-sour caramelised onions provide the perfect balance in this main course pasta dish.

60 ml (4 tbsp) extra-virgin olive oil, plus extra for brushing

2 small red onions, peeled and thinly sliced

1 garlic clove, peeled and crushed

15 ml (1 tbsp) chopped fresh thyme

pinch of sugar

2 heads of radicchio, cut into thick wedges

1 quantity fresh buckwheat tagliatelle (see page 11), or 400 g (14 oz) dried (see note)

salt and pepper

30 ml (2 tbsp) balsamic vinegar

25 g (1 oz) capers in wine vinegar, drained

50 g (2 oz) pine nuts, toasted

30 ml (2 tbsp) chopped fresh basil

basil leaves, to garnish

freshly grated Parmesan cheese, to taste (optional)

1 Heat the 60 ml (4 tbsp) oil in a deep frying pan, add the onions, garlic, thyme and sugar and fry for 10-15 minutes until golden and tender.
2 Meanwhile, preheat the grill. Lay the radicchio wedges on the grill rack, brush with a little oil and grill for 2-3 minutes. Turn the wedges over, brush with oil and grill for a further 2-3 minutes until charred and tender; keep warm.
3 Cook the buckwheat pasta in a large pan of boiling salted water until *al dente*; fresh pasta will only take 1-2 minutes.
4 Add the balsamic vinegar, capers, nuts and basil to the onions and stir well; keep warm.
5 Drain the pasta, reserving 60 ml (4 tbsp) water. Add both to the onions with the radicchio. Stir briefly over a medium heat, then season with salt and pepper. Serve at once, garnished with basil and accompanied by Parmesan, if wished.

NOTE: If using dried pasta, which takes 10-12 minutes to cook, start cooking before grilling the radicchio.

Tagliatelle with Broad Beans, Chicory and Cream

Serves 4
Preparation 25 minutes
Cooking 10 minutes
880-590 calories per serving

Tender, bright green broad beans and chicory are tossed in a creamy sauce, with herbs, and served with tagliatelle and Parmesan.

350 g (12 oz) frozen broad beans, thawed

40 g (1½ oz) butter

1 onion, peeled and finely chopped

400 g (14 oz) dried white and green tagliatelle or freshly made tagliatelle

2 heads chicory, about 200 g (7 oz) total weight, sliced

45 ml (3 tbsp) chopped fresh parsley or chervil

300 ml (½ pint) extra-thick double cream

60 ml (4 tbsp) freshly grated Parmesan cheese

salt and pepper

TO SERVE

extra herbs and Parmesan cheese

1 Slip the broad beans out of their outer skins and place in a bowl; set aside.
2 Melt the butter in a large frying pan. Add the onion and cook over a medium heat, stirring frequently, for 5-6 minutes until soft.
3 Cook the pasta in a large pan of boiling salted water until *al dente*.
4 Meanwhile, add the broad beans to the onion in the frying pan and continue cooking for 2 minutes, then stir in the chicory and parsley or chervil. Cook for a further 2 minutes, then stir in the cream. Bring to the boil and add the grated Parmesan. Season with salt and pepper to taste.
5 Drain the pasta thoroughly and toss with the sauce. Serve at once, sprinkled with extra herbs and shavings of Parmesan cheese.

Penne with Red Cabbage, Soured Cream and Walnuts

Serves 4-6
Preparation 25 minutes
Cooking 10-15 minutes
630-420 calories per serving

This unusual pasta dish makes an excellent main course for a cold winter's day. The secret of its success lies in shredding the red cabbage very finely, to ensure that it cooks quickly, retaining its texture.

45 ml (3 tbsp) extra-virgin olive oil

1 large red onion, peeled and finely sliced

700 g (1½ lb) red cabbage, cored, seeded and finely shredded

2 garlic cloves, peeled and crushed

175 g (6 oz) dried pasta shapes, such as penne or shells

salt and pepper

1 Granny Smith apple (unpeeled), cored and finely diced

juice of 1 large orange

30 ml (2 tbsp) balsamic vinegar

300 ml (½ pint) soured cream

TO GARNISH

30 ml (2 tbsp) walnut oil

50 g (2 oz) walnut halves

100 g (3½ oz) goat's cheese log or feta cheese, diced

chopped oregano, to taste

1 Heat the olive oil in a heavy-based, wide sauté pan, add the onion and fry gently for about 5 minutes, until softened but not coloured. Add the cabbage and garlic and stir-fry for about 5 minutes.

2 Cook the pasta in a large pan of boiling salted water until *al dente*.

3 When the cabbage begins to wilt, add the apple, orange juice and 60 ml (4 tbsp) water. Continue to stir-fry for a further 5 minutes. Increase the heat slightly, pour in the balsamic vinegar and cook, stirring, until the cabbage is *al dente* and only a little liquid remains. Season with salt and pepper to taste. Remove from the heat and keep warm.

4 Meanwhile, heat the walnut oil in a small frying pan over a high heat, add the walnuts and fry for 2 minutes.

5 Drain the pasta and toss with the cabbage and apple mixture, and the soured cream. Serve at once, topped with the walnuts in oil, diced cheese and oregano.

Pasta Bake with Roasted Vegetables

Serves 8
Preparation 35 minutes
Cooking 1½ hours
585 calories per serving

Roasting brings out the full flavour of aubergines, peppers and squash. Here, these vegetables are first roasted, then tossed with pasta, spinach and a cheesy sauce, and finally baked under a cheesy crust.

450 g (1 lb) aubergines

700 g (1½ lb) mixed peppers, halved, cored and seeded

450 g (1 lb) squash, such as butternut or pumpkin, peeled and seeded

90 ml (6 tbsp) olive oil

225 g (8 oz) dried pasta shapes, such as shells or penne

salt and pepper

50 g (2 oz) butter

50 g (2 oz) plain white flour

900 ml (1½ pints) milk

30 ml (2 tbsp) wholegrain mustard

150 g (5 oz) soft cheese with garlic and herbs, such as Boursin

225 g (8 oz) mature Cheddar cheese, grated

450 g (1 lb) frozen leaf spinach, thawed and drained

1 Preheat the oven to 220°C (425°F) Mark 7. Cut the aubergines, peppers and squash into bite-sized pieces and place in a single layer in two roasting tins. Drizzle with the oil. Roast in the oven until tender and charred. Reduce the setting to 200°C (400°F) Mark 6.

2 Cook the pasta in a large pan of boiling salted water until *al dente*.

3 Meanwhile, make the sauce. Melt the butter in a pan, stir in the flour and cook, stirring, for 1 minute. Gradually stir in the milk, then bring to the boil, stirring all the time. Simmer for 2-3 minutes or until smooth and thickened. Off the heat, add the mustard, soft cheese and all but 50 g (2 oz) of the Cheddar. Stir thoroughly until smooth. Season well.

4 Drain the pasta thoroughly. Toss with the sauce, spinach and roasted

vegetables. Spoon into a large shallow ovenproof dish and sprinkle over the remaining Cheddar cheese.

5 Stand the dish on a baking sheet. Bake in the oven for about 40 minutes or until golden brown and bubbling, covering the top with foil, if necessary, to prevent over-browning.

NOTE: If required, this dish may be frozen at the end of stage 4. Defrost thoroughly at room temperature before baking.

Tortelloni with Spiced Nut Sauce

Serves 4
Preparation 30 minutes
Cooking About 10 minutes
1090 calories per serving

Use your favourite ready-made or freshly prepared tortelloni for this sustaining supper dish. Alternatively, you can toss the sauce with ribbon pasta and serve as a tasty accompaniment to grilled vegetables or trout. The sauce is quick and easy to make and can be stored in the refrigerator for up to 1 week.

500 g (1 lb 2 oz) fresh tortelloni (of your choice)

SAUCE
50 g (2 oz) walnut pieces
50 g (2 oz) hazelnuts
50 g (2 oz) brazil nuts, roughly chopped
1 large onion, peeled and roughly chopped
1 garlic clove, peeled and roughly chopped
2.5 cm (1 inch) piece fresh root ginger, peeled and roughly chopped

30 ml (2 tbsp) ground coriander
10 ml (2 tsp) ground cardamom seeds (from 12 pods)
5 ml (1 tsp) chilli powder
300 ml (½ pint) double cream
75 g (3 oz) raisins
juice of 1 lemon, or to taste
salt and pepper

TO GARNISH
30-45 ml (3-4 tbsp) chopped fresh coriander leaves

1 Preheat the oven to 200°C (400°F) Mark 6. To prepare the sauce, spread the nuts on a baking sheet and toast in the oven for about 10 minutes, until pale golden brown; watch carefully as they will burn quickly. Allow to cool.
2 When the nuts are cold, chop coarsely using a food processor. Set aside 30 ml (2 tbsp) for the garnish. Add the onion, garlic, ginger and spices to the food processor and work until smooth.
3 Transfer the nut mixture to a saucepan, add the cream and season well. Bring to the boil and simmer over a moderate heat for about 10 minutes until reduced and slightly thickened.
4 Meanwhile, cook the tortelloni in a large saucepan of boiling salted water for about 6-8 minutes or until *al dente*.
5 Stir the raisins into the sauce, then add lemon juice to taste and check the seasoning. Drain the pasta and toss with the sauce. Serve garnished with the reserved toasted nuts and plenty of chopped coriander.

Tortelloni with Roasted Squash and Sage Butter

Serves 4 (or 6 as a starter)
Preparation 40 minutes, plus pasta and chilling
Cooking 23 minutes
655-640 calories per serving

Illustrated opposite

An irresistible combination of flavours makes these sweet little parcels the perfect pasta dish for a special occasion. Serve them as a starter, or main dish if you prefer.

300 g (10 oz) butternut squash, peeled and seeded (ie 225 g (8 oz) flesh), cubed
1 garlic clove, peeled and crushed
10 ml (2 tsp) chopped fresh thyme
30 ml (2 tbsp) olive oil
75 g (3 oz) ricotta cheese
25 g (1 oz) Parmesan cheese, freshly grated
pinch of freshly grated nutmeg

squeeze of lemon juice
salt and pepper
1 quantity fresh pasta dough (see page 10)
125 g (4 oz) unsalted butter, softened
30 ml (2 tbsp) chopped fresh sage leaves
freshly grated Parmesan, to serve (optional)

1 Preheat the oven to 225°C (425°F) Mark 7. Place the cubed squash in a small roasting pan with the garlic, thyme and oil. Toss well and roast in the oven for 20 minutes until softened. Mash with a potato masher and set aside to cool.

2 Transfer the cooled squash purée to a bowl and beat in the ricotta, Parmesan, nutmeg, lemon juice and seasoning. Cover and chill for 30 minutes.

3 Divide the dough into 8 pieces and roll out each one, using a pasta machine if possible, to a thin sheet (see page 12). Keep all except one of the pasta sheets covered with cling film. Using a plain 6 cm (2½ inch) pastry cutter, stamp out 6 rounds from the single pasta sheet.

4 Place 5 ml (1 tsp) of the squash mixture in the middle of each round. Brush the edge of one half of each round with water, then fold the other half over to enclose the filling. Press the edges together to seal well.

5 Curve the semi-circular parcel around your finger and pinch the ends together, turning the sealed edge up to form a neat curved tortelloni as you do so. Place on a well floured tea-towel. Repeat with the remaining pasta and filling to make 48 tortelloni.

6 Cook the tortelloni in a large pan of boiling salted water for 2-3 minutes until *al dente*. Drain well.

7 At the same time, melt the butter with the sage in a large frying pan until foaming. Add the tortelloni and toss well. Serve at once with black pepper, and Parmesan if wished.

NOTE: If rolling the pasta dough by hand, divide into 4 pieces and roll out on a floured surface as thinly as possible. Stamp out 12 rounds from each sheet.

The tortelloni may be frozen at the end of stage 5. Thaw at room temperature before cooking as above.

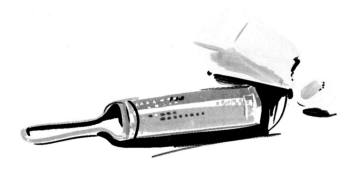

Classic Vegetable Lasagne

Serves 6
Preparation 40 minutes
Cooking 45 minutes-1 hour
285 calories per serving

Sheets of fresh lasagne are available from the chilled cabinet of most supermarkets these days. If using pre-cooked dried lasagne sheets, add a little extra liquid (stock or water) to the vegetable mixture. Serve with a crisp green salad.

30 ml (2 tbsp) olive oil
1 garlic clove, peeled and crushed
1 carrot, peeled and chopped
1 large onion, peeled and sliced
1 red pepper, cored, seeded and chopped
15 ml (1 tbsp) mild paprika
10 ml (2 tsp) dried oregano or marjoram
1 large aubergine, cut into large chunks
225 g (8 oz) button mushrooms, sliced
2 large courgettes, sliced
two 400 g (14 oz) cans chopped tomatoes
30 ml (2 tbsp) tomato purée
2 bay leaves

BÉCHAMEL SAUCE
900 ml (1½ pints) milk
2 onion slices
2 bay leaves
6 peppercorns
2 mace blades
40 g (1½ oz) butter
40 g (1½ oz) plain white flour
about 350 g (12 oz) fresh lasagne or 225 g (8 oz) dried
salt and pepper

TO FINISH
Parmesan or Cheddar cheese, freshly grated (optional)

1 Heat the oil in a large saucepan. Add the garlic, carrot, onion and pepper and fry for 1-2 minutes or until beginning to soften. Add the paprika, herbs and aubergine and fry for a few minutes longer.

2 Add the remaining vegetables to the pan with the tomatoes, tomato purée and bay leaves. Bring to the boil, then reduce the heat, cover and simmer for 30 minutes.

3 Meanwhile, make the béchamel sauce. Put the milk in a saucepan with the onion, bay leaves, peppercorns and mace, and bring almost to the boil. Take off the heat, cover and leave to infuse for 20 minutes. Melt the butter in a pan. Stir in the flour and cook, stirring, for 1-2 minutes. Gradually stir in the milk, then bring to the boil, stirring constantly. Simmer, stirring, for 2-3 minutes or until smooth and thickened.

4 Preheat the oven to 200°C (400°F) Mark 6. Meanwhile, if using dried lasagne that needs pre-cooking, cook in boiling salted water according to packet instructions. Drain and leave to dry on a clean tea-towel.

5 Spread a small amount of the tomato sauce in the base of a 2.8 litre (5 pint) ovenproof dish. Cover with a layer of lasagne and top with a layer of béchamel sauce. Continue layering in this way, ending with a layer of béchamel sauce that covers the pasta completely. Sprinkle with the cheese, if using.

6 Bake in the oven for 45 minutes-1 hour or until well browned and piping hot. Leave to stand for 15 minutes before serving.

NOTE: If required, the lasagne may be frozen at the end of stage 5. Defrost thoroughly at room temperature prior to baking.

Vegetarian Lasagne with Goat Cheese Topping

Serves 6
Preparation About 1 hour
Cooking 40 minutes
685 calories per serving

This vegetarian lasagne has a rich Mediterranean vegetable filling complemented by a set custard-like topping made from goat's cheese, eggs and cream. Use the mild soft young goat's cheese – *chèvre frais* – which is usually sold in tubs. Alternatively you can use cream cheese or curd cheese instead.

4 red, orange or yellow peppers
2 medium aubergines, cut into 1 cm (½ inch) cubes
salt and pepper
75 ml (5 tbsp) extra-virgin olive oil
2 onions, peeled and chopped
4 garlic cloves, peeled and thinly sliced
75 ml (5 tbsp) red wine or water
45 ml (3 tbsp) chopped fresh oregano
90 ml (6 tbsp) sun-dried tomato paste

12 sheets dried lasagne

TOPPING
350 g (12 oz) fresh soft goat's cheese
2 eggs
150 ml (¼ pint) single cream
45 ml (3 tbsp) day-old white breadcrumbs
30 ml (2 tbsp) freshly grated Parmesan cheese

1 Preheat the grill to hot. Place the whole peppers on the grill rack and grill, turning from time to time, until the skins are blackened and blistered all over. This will take about 20 minutes. Allow to cool slightly, then over a bowl to catch the juices, remove the skins. Chop the flesh, discarding the seeds: set aside with the juices.

2 Meanwhile, put the diced aubergines in a colander, rinse, then sprinkle liberally with salt. Leave for 20 minutes, to extract the bitter juices. Rinse again, then blanch in boiling water for 1 minute; drain well.

3 Heat the oil in a large saucepan. Add the onions and cook, stirring frequently, for about 8 minutes until soft and golden. Add the garlic and cook for a further 2 minutes. Add the wine and allow to bubble for 1 minute, then stir in the aubergine, oregano and sun-dried tomato paste. Cover and cook over a medium heat for 15-20 minutes, stirring frequently. Remove from the heat and stir in the grilled peppers and seasoning.

4 Preheat the oven to 190°C (375°F) Mark 5. Cook the lasagne in a large pan of boiling salted water until *al dente* or according to packet instructions. Drain, then drop into a bowl of cold water with 30 ml (2 tbsp) oil added to prevent the sheets from sticking. Drain again and lay on a clean tea towel.

5 Oil a baking dish, measuring about 25 x 18 x 8 cm (10 x 7 x 3½ inches). Spread one third of the filling in the base and then cover with a layer of pasta, trimming to fit the dish as necessary. Add another third of the filling and cover with pasta as before. Cover with the last of the filling and arrange the remaining pasta sheets over the top.

6 To make the topping, place the goat's cheese in a bowl, add the eggs and beat well. Stir in the cream and seasoning. Pour over the lasagne and spread evenly. Sprinkle with the breadcrumbs and Parmesan, then bake in the oven for about 35-40 minutes, until heated through and lightly browned on top.

NOTE: If required, the lasagne may be frozen at the end of stage 5. Defrost thoroughly at room temperature before baking.

VARIATION
Replace the goat's cheese topping with 350 g (12 oz) mozzarella, sliced.

Pasta with Mediterranean Vegetables and Walnut Paste

Serves 4-6
Preparation 25 minutes
Cooking 20 minutes
950-630 calories per serving

Illustrated opposite

Pasta tossed in walnut paste is a wonderful combination and a delicious dish in its own right. Topped with grilled Mediterranean vegetables it makes a gutsy, colourful dish.

1 fennel bulb, sliced
2 small red onions, peeled and cut into wedges
2 courgettes, halved and thinly sliced lengthwise
1 large red pepper, cored, seeded and cut into broad strips
6 small tomatoes, halved
45 ml (3 tbsp) extra-virgin olive oil
15 ml (1 tbsp) chopped fresh thyme
5 ml (1 tsp) grated lemon rind
400 g (14 oz) dried tagliatelle
coarse sea salt and pepper

WALNUT PASTE
150 g (5 oz) walnuts, roughly chopped
1 garlic clove, peeled and chopped
45 ml (3 tbsp) chopped fresh parsley
75 ml (5 tbsp) extra-virgin olive oil
50 g (2 oz) ricotta or other soft cheese

TO GARNISH
thyme sprigs

1 Add the fennel and onions to a large pan of boiling water, bring back to the boil and cook for 2 minutes. Add the courgette strips and cook for a further 1 minute. Drain in a colander and refresh under cold running water. Drain and set aside.

2 Preheat the grill to high. Put the blanched vegetables in a bowl with the red pepper and tomatoes. Add the olive oil, thyme and lemon rind and toss to coat.

3 Transfer the vegetables to the foil-lined grill pan and grill for 15-20 minutes, turning occasionally until they are tender and patched with brown.

4 Meanwhile, cook the tagliatelle in a large pan of boiling salted water until *al dente*.

5 Meanwhile, prepare the walnut paste. Put the walnuts and garlic into a food processor and process briefly to chop finely. Add the parsley and process for 1 second. Add the oil and work to a coarse paste. Transfer to a bowl and stir in the ricotta and seasoning.

6 Drain the pasta thoroughly in a colander. Meanwhile, gently heat the walnut paste in the large pasta pan for a few seconds, then remove from the heat, add the pasta and toss to mix. Serve at once, topped with the grilled vegetables, drizzling over any oil and juices from the grill pan.

VARIATION
Use olive paste rather than walnut paste. Either buy ready-made olive paste or make your own, by processing stoned olives with a chopped garlic clove, olive oil and some chopped herbs.

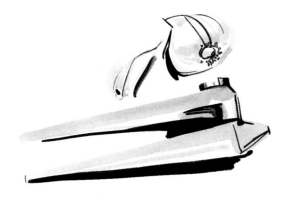

Spaghettini and Almond 'Rösti'

Serves 4
Preparation 20 minutes
Cooking 30 minutes
475 calories per serving

Illustrated opposite

Here is an unusual but delicious way of presenting pasta. Spaghettini is flavoured with onions, toasted almonds and crushed spices, then packed into a 'cake' and fried to a light crisp crust. Served with a refreshing mango, red pepper and ginger relish, this makes an interesting starter or light main course.

50 g (2 oz) flaked almonds
90 ml (6 tbsp) oil
2 medium onions, thinly sliced
1 garlic clove, crushed
150 g (5 oz) spaghettini or paglia e fieno
salt and pepper
60 ml (4 tbsp) chopped fresh coriander
10 ml (2 tsp) cumin seeds, crushed
40 g (1½ oz) ground almonds

MANGO RELISH
1 large, ripe mango, peeled, stoned and finely chopped
5 g (¼ oz) preserved stem ginger, finely chopped, plus 15 ml (1 tbsp) syrup from the jar
¼ red pepper, seeded and diced
10-15 ml (2-3 tsp) white wine vinegar

TO GARNISH
lemon wedges
chopped coriander

1 First make the relish. Lightly mash the chopped mango flesh in a bowl to give a more pulpy texture. Add the chopped ginger with the syrup, red pepper, seasoning and vinegar to taste. Mix well, then transfer to a serving dish; cover and chill.

2 Toast the almonds in a medium, non-stick frying pan, then remove from the pan and set aside. Heat 30 ml (2 tbsp) oil in the pan, add the onions and garlic, and fry gently for about 12 minutes until very soft.

3 Meanwhile, add the pasta to a large pan of boiling salted water and cook until *al dente*.

4 Drain the pasta and toss with the onions, toasted almonds, coriander, cumin, ground almonds and seasoning until thoroughly combined.

5 Heat 30 ml (2 tbsp) oil in the frying pan. Turn the pasta mixture into the pan and spread to an even layer, scattering any ingredients left in the bowl over the surface. Pack the mixture down lightly and cook gently for 12 minutes until the underside is golden.

6 Carefully invert the cake onto a baking sheet. Heat the remaining 30 ml (2 tbsp) of the oil in the pan. Slide the pasta back into the pan and fry gently for another 5 minutes.

7 Cut the 'rösti' into wedges. Serve with the mango relish, lemon wedges and a scattering of coriander.

NOTE: The relish and rösti mixture can be prepared ahead to the end of stage 4, ready for last-minute cooking.

VARIATION
Divide the rösti mixture into 4 portions and shape into individual cakes. Cook as above, pressing well down. Serve garnished with coriander sprigs.

Pasta and Aubergine Gratin

Serves 4
Preparation 15 minutes
Cooking 20 minutes
565 calories per serving

Serve this tasty gratin as a mid-week family supper with warm crusty bread and a crisp leafy salad.

30 ml (2 tbsp) olive oil
1 onion, peeled and chopped
1 garlic clove, peeled and crushed
10 ml (2 tsp) mild paprika
10 ml (2 tsp) tomato purée
350 g (12 oz) aubergine, roughly chopped
400 g (14 oz) can chopped tomatoes
5 ml (1 tsp) sugar
2 small courgettes, thinly sliced
salt and pepper
275 g (10 oz) dried rigatoni or other pasta shapes
15 ml (1 tbsp) pesto
150 g (5 oz) Gruyère or mature Cheddar cheese
25 g (1 oz) freshly grated Parmesan cheese

1 Preheat the oven to 200°C (400°F) Mark 6. Heat the oil in a heavy-based saucepan, add the onion and garlic and fry until softened. Add the paprika and tomato purée and cook, stirring, for 1 minute. Add the aubergine and cook for a further 2 minutes, stirring to coat in the tomato and onion mixture.
2 Add the tomatoes, sugar and 75 ml (5 tbsp) water. Bring to the boil, then cover, reduce the heat and simmer for about 15 minutes or until the aubergine is just tender. Add the courgettes, re-cover and cook for a further 5 minutes. Season with salt and pepper to taste.
3 Meanwhile, cook the pasta in a large pan of boiling salted water until *al dente*, return to the pan and toss with the pesto.
4 Toss the pasta with the aubergine sauce and check the seasoning. Transfer to an ovenproof dish and top with the grated cheeses. Bake in the oven for about 20 minutes until golden brown and bubbling.

Spinach and Ricotta Ravioli

Serves 4
Preparation 20 minutes, plus pasta
Cooking 3 minutes
525 calories per serving

A delicate filling of spinach and ricotta cheese, seasoned with nutmeg and pepper, is enveloped by fresh egg pasta and served tossed in melted butter. Slivers of freshly pared Parmesan complete this simple but delicious dish.

1 quantity fresh pasta (see page 10)
FILLING
300 g (10 oz) frozen spinach, thawed and squeezed dry
125 g (4 oz) fresh ricotta or curd cheese
1.25 ml (¼ tsp) freshly grated nutmeg
2.5 ml (½ tsp) salt
pepper, to taste

TO FINISH
beaten egg, to seal
75 g (3 oz) butter, melted
25 g (1 oz) Parmesan cheese, freshly pared

1 Wrap the pasta in cling film and allow to rest at room temperature for at least 30 minutes before rolling out.
2 To make the filling, place all the ingredients in a food processor or blender and process until smooth. Cover and refrigerate.
3 If using a pasta machine, roll manageable portions of dough into strips. If rolling out by hand, cut the dough in half and re-wrap one piece in cling film. Roll the other piece out thinly on a lightly floured surface to a rectangle and cover with a clean damp tea-towel. Repeat with the remaining pasta.
4 Spoon or pipe small mounds of filling, in even rows across one half of the dough, spacing them at 4 cm (1½ inch) intervals. Brush the spaces of dough between the mounds with beaten egg. Using a rolling pin, carefully lift the other sheet(s) of pasta over the top. Press down firmly between the pockets of filling, pushing out any trapped air.
5 Cut into squares, using a serrated ravioli cutter or sharp knife. Transfer to a floured tea-towel and leave to rest for 1 hour before cooking.
6 Bring a large saucepan of salted water to the boil. Add the ravioli and cook

for about 3 minutes, until puffy. Drain well and toss with the melted butter. Serve topped with slivers of Parmesan.

VARIATION
For a non-vegetarian filling, sauté 125 g (4 oz) chopped pancetta or thick-cut unsmoked bacon in butter until golden and crisp. Stir in 45 ml (3 tbsp) chopped fresh sage. Allow to cool, then beat into the ricotta filling. Continue as above.

Herbed Mushroom Ravioli

Serves 6 as a starter
Preparation 25 minutes, plus pasta
Cooking 5 minutes
550 calories per serving

These pretty green herb-speckled ravioli are filled with a delicious mixture of wild mushrooms. Serve them simply topped with melted butter and freshly pared Parmesan cheese, as a sophisticated starter.

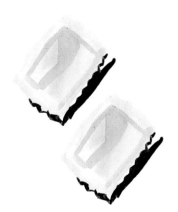

1 quantity fresh herb pasta (see page 10)

MUSHROOM FILLING
225 g (8 oz) mixed wild mushrooms or 175 g (6 oz) dark flat mushrooms, plus 40 g (1½ oz) dried porcini
50 g (2 oz) butter
2 shallots, peeled and finely chopped
25 g (1 oz) black olives, stoned and finely chopped

4 sun-dried tomatoes in oil, drained and finely chopped
15 ml (1 tbsp) dry sherry
salt and pepper
freshly grated nutmeg
beaten egg, for brushing

TO SERVE
50 g (2 oz) butter, melted
few sautéed wild mushrooms
freshly pared Parmesan cheese

1 Wrap the pasta in cling film and allow to rest at room temperature for 30 minutes.
2 To prepare the filling, wipe or brush the fresh mushrooms clean, then chop finely. If using dried mushrooms, soak in hot water to cover for 10-15 minutes. Remove and chop finely. Strain the soaking liquid through a filter paper to remove any grit and reserve.
3 Melt the butter in a pan, add the shallots and cook for 5 minutes until soft and golden. Add all the mushrooms, olives and sun-dried tomatoes; cook, stirring, over a high heat for 1-2 minutes. Add the sherry and reserved liquid; cook for 1 minute. Season well with salt, pepper and nutmeg. Transfer to a bowl; allow to cool.
4 If using a pasta machine, roll manageable portions of dough into strips. If rolling out by hand, divide in half and roll into 2 sheets on a very lightly floured surface. Either way, roll out as thinly as possible and keep covered with a slightly damp tea towel.
5 Place 18 heaped spoonfuls of filling on one half of the pasta, spacing them at 4 cm (1½ inch) intervals. Brush the dough in between with beaten egg. Lift the other sheet(s) of pasta over the top. Press down firmly between the pockets of filling and cut into 7.5 cm (3 inch) squares. Transfer to a floured tea-towel and leave to rest for 1 hour.
6 Bring a large pan of salted water to the boil, with a dash of oil added. Carefully add the ravioli, bring back to the boil, turn off the heat and cover with a tight-fitting lid. Leave for 5 minutes, then drain well. Serve immediately, on warmed plates, topped with the melted butter, sautéed mushrooms and shavings of Parmesan cheese.

NOTE: The ravioli may be frozen at the end of stage 5. Defrost thoroughly before cooking.

PASTA SALADS

Chicken, Cashew and Noodle Salad

Serves 4
Preparation 25 minutes, plus marinating
Cooking 4-5 minutes
470 calories per serving

Illustrated opposite

Spicy fried strips of chicken, crisp green vegetables, herbs and toasted cashew nuts are tossed with noodles in a tangy soy dressing to create a delicious salad. If time permits, allow the chicken to marinate for several hours for optimum flavour.

350 g (12 oz) skinless chicken breast fillet
30 ml (2 tbsp) sunflower oil
5 ml (1 tsp) sesame oil
5 ml (1 tsp) ground coriander
1.25 ml (¼ tsp) chilli powder
pinch of Chinese five-spice powder
125 g (4 oz) dried egg noodles (½ packet)
50 g (2 oz) mangetouts
50 g (2 oz) French beans, halved
15 ml (1 tbsp) chopped fresh mint
15 ml (1 tbsp) chopped fresh coriander

DRESSING
45 ml (3 tbsp) peanut or sunflower oil
10 ml (2 tsp) sesame oil
1 garlic clove, peeled and crushed
5 ml (1 tsp) grated fresh root ginger
2.5 ml (½ tsp) dried red chilli flakes, crushed
15 ml (1 tbsp) dark soy sauce
15 ml (1 tbsp) lemon juice

TO GARNISH
25 g (1 oz) cashew nuts, toasted
coriander sprigs

1 Very thinly slice the chicken breast, across the grain, then place in a shallow non-reactive dish. Combine 15 ml (1 tbsp) of the sunflower oil with the sesame oil, coriander, chilli powder and Chinese five-spice powder. Add to the chicken and stir until evenly coated. Cover and leave to marinate for at least 30 minutes.
2 Cook the noodles according to the packet instructions.
3 Heat the remaining sunflower oil in a large non-stick frying pan. When hot, add the marinated chicken pieces and stir-fry for 2 minutes until golden and crispy. Drain on kitchen paper.
4 Add the vegetables and herbs to the pan and stir-fry for 1 minute until tender. Add to the chicken pieces and keep warm.
5 To make the dressing, heat both oils in a small pan, add the garlic, ginger and chilli flakes and fry gently until softened but not coloured. Whisk in the soy sauce, lemon juice and 30 ml (2 tbsp) water. Bring to the boil and remove from the heat.
6 Drain the cooked noodles and immediately toss with the hot soy dressing and chicken and vegetable mixture. Sprinkle over the toasted cashews. Serve warm or cool, garnished with coriander.

VARIATION
Replace the chicken with the same weight of peeled, raw tiger prawns and add 10 ml (2 tsp) grated lime to the marinade. Stir-fry for 3-4 minutes until the prawns have turned pink. Use basil instead of mint and replace the lemon juice in the dressing with lime juice.

Hot and Sour Noodle and Vegetable Salad

Serves 4
Preparation 30 minutes, plus optional chilling
Cooking 3-4 minutes
345 calories per serving

For this tempting salad, transparent rice vermicelli noodles are tossed in a spicy lime dressing, together with a colourful selection of crispy fried vegetables. Serve warm, or slightly chilled if preferred.

30 ml (2 tbsp) peanut or sunflower oil
15 ml (1 tbsp) sesame oil
2 garlic cloves, peeled and crushed
5 ml (1 tsp) dried red chilli flakes, crushed
5 ml (1 tsp) grated fresh root ginger
2 carrots, peeled and cut into julienne
50 g (2 oz) baby sweetcorn, halved lengthwise
50 g (2 oz) mangetouts, trimmed
50 g (2 oz) broccoli, divided into small florets
1 small red pepper, cored, seeded and thinly sliced
125 g (4 oz) Chinese cabbage or pak choi, roughly shredded
50 g (2 oz) canned water chestnuts, drained and sliced
75 g (3 oz) rice vermicelli noodles
30 ml (2 tbsp) chopped fresh coriander

DRESSING
30 ml (2 tbsp) peanut oil
5 ml (1 tsp) chilli oil
10 ml (2 tsp) caster sugar
30 ml (2 tbsp) lime juice
15 ml (1 tbsp) rice vinegar
15 ml (1 tbsp) Thai fish sauce
salt and pepper

TO GARNISH
25 g (1 oz) raw peanuts, toasted and chopped

1 Heat the two oils in a small pan, together with the garlic, chilli flakes and ginger, until smoking. Strain the oil into a wok or large frying pan and place over a high heat.

2 Add the prepared vegetables and waterchestnuts; stir-fry for 2-3 minutes until just beginning to wilt. Immediately remove the pan from the heat.

3 Cook the noodles according to the packet instructions. Meanwhile, whisk all the dressing ingredients together, seasoning with salt and pepper to taste. Strain the cooked noodles and toss with a little of the dressing.

4 Stir the remaining dressing into the vegetables together with the chopped coriander. Arrange the noodles and vegetables on individual serving plates. Scatter over the toasted peanuts and serve at once or chill for up to 1 hour before serving if preferred.

VARIATION
Include some deep-fried tofu. Cut 125 g (4 oz) plain tofu into cubes and dry well. Deep-fry in hot oil for 2-3 minutes until crisp and golden. Add to the vegetables and noodles just before serving.

Warm Pasta Salad with Garlic and Serrano

Serves 4
Preparation 15 minutes
Cooking About 15 minutes
715 calories per serving

8 large garlic cloves
150 g (5 oz) crème fraîche
7 g (¼ oz) chopped fresh basil leaves
salt and pepper
120 ml (8 tbsp) extra-virgin olive oil
1 onion, peeled and thinly sliced
1 medium aubergine, thinly sliced
225 g (8 oz) dried pasta shells
25 g (1 oz) flaked almonds, toasted
30 ml (2 tbsp) balsamic vinegar
60 g (2½ oz) Serrano or Parma ham, torn into pieces
freshly grated nutmeg, to taste
basil leaves, to garnish
freshly pared Parmesan cheese, to serve (optional)

1 Peel and crush 1 garlic clove and mix with the crème fraîche, basil and seasoning. Spoon into a serving dish and set aside.

2 Peel and halve the remaining garlic and blanch in boiling water for 2 minutes.

3 Heat 15 ml (1 tbsp) of the oil in a large frying pan, add the onion and fry

A simple combination of aubergine, smoked ham, almonds and basil spiked with plenty of garlicky, olive oil juices and served topped with a basil-flavoured crème fraîche. The topping melts deliciously onto the warm pasta, making a refreshingly light, summer salad. If liked, scatter the salad with slivers of freshly grated Parmesan before serving.

quickly until charred. Remove with a slotted spoon and set aside. Add a little more oil to the pan and fry half of the aubergine slices and garlic, turning once, until the aubergines are golden on both sides. Drain and repeat with the remaining aubergine and garlic.

4 Cook the pasta in a large pan of boiling salted water until *al dente*.

5 Drain the pasta thoroughly and toss with the onion, aubergine and garlic, toasted almonds, vinegar, seasoning and any remaining oil.

6 Spoon onto serving plates and scatter the ham over each portion. Season with salt, pepper and a little nutmeg. Garnish with basil leaves and add the crème fraîche topping. Serve warm, topped with Parmesan if desired.

Warm Duck and Pasta Salad with Dried Cherries

Serves 4
Preparation 15 minutes
Cooking 25 minutes
810 calories per serving

Illustrated on page 145

This interesting combination of flavours is visually stunning. Duck has a particular affinity with fruit, and the sweet sour taste of the dried cherries cuts the richness of the duck beautifully. The balsamic dressing adds a piquancy too.

2 duck breasts, each about 225 g (8 oz)
300 g (10 oz) dried pasta, such as torchiette
50 g (2 oz) dried cherries
175 g (6 oz) French beans, trimmed and halved
50 g (2 oz) walnut pieces

30 ml (2 tbsp) chopped fresh chives

DRESSING
125 ml (4 fl oz) olive oil
15 ml (1 tbsp) balsamic vinegar
5 ml (1 tsp) sugar
salt and pepper

1 Score the skin of the duck breasts in a criss-cross fashion.

2 For the dressing, mix together the oil, balsamic vinegar, sugar and seasoning.

3 Preheat a heavy-based frying pan or cast-iron griddle. When it is really hot, add the duck breasts, skin-side down, and cook for 10 minutes, pouring off the fat as it melts away. Turn the duck breasts over and cook for a further 3 minutes. Remove and set aside until cool enough to handle.

4 In the meantime, cook the pasta in a large pan of boiling salted water until *al dente*.

5 Meanwhile, cook the French beans in boiling salted water for 3-4 minutes, until just tender. Drain and refresh under cold water.

6 Drain the pasta thoroughly and place in a large bowl. Add the dressing and toss to mix.

7 Thinly slice the duck and add to the pasta with the dried cherries, French beans, walnuts and chives. Check the seasoning, toss well and serve warm.

NOTE: If preferred, this salad may be served at room temperature: after cooking the pasta refresh under cold water before tossing with the other ingredients.

VARIATIONS
If dried cherries are unavailable, use raisins, sultanas, dried cranberries or dried blueberries instead.

Pasta Salad with Squid, Fennel and Tomato

Serves 4
Preparation 20 minutes, plus pasta
Cooking 10 minutes
720 calories per serving

This summery combination of squid, fennel and pasta, tossed in a tangy tomato sauce makes a tempting main course salad. For convenience, ready-cleaned squid tubes can be used instead of whole squid, but you won't get the tentacles, which always add colour and interest.

450 g (1 lb) small squid
15 ml (1 tbsp) plain flour, for coating
salt and pepper
5 ripe plum tomatoes, skinned, seeded and diced
4 garlic cloves, peeled and crushed
1 red chilli, seeded and sliced
finely pared rind of 1 lemon

30 ml (2 tbsp) lemon juice
45 ml (3 tbsp) balsamic vinegar
2.5 ml (½ tsp) caster sugar
120 ml (8 tbsp) olive oil
2 small fennel bulbs, thinly sliced
1 quantity fresh pasta (see page 10) or 350 g (12 oz) dried pasta shapes
fennel sprigs and lemon wedges, to garnish

1 Pull the squid tentacles and pouch apart. Cut the tentacles away from the head, just below the eyes; discard the head. Squeeze out and discard the contents of the pouch, including the plastic-like quill. Peel off the thin layer of skin. Wash the pouches and tentacles and dry well. Slice the pouches into rings. Toss the squid in seasoned flour to coat, shaking off excess.
2 Put the diced tomatoes in a bowl with the garlic, chilli, lemon rind and juice, vinegar, sugar, 90 ml (6 tbsp) of the oil and seasoning.
3 Heat the remaining oil in a heavy-based frying pan. Add the fennel and fry quickly over a high heat until charred; remove and set aside. Add the squid to the pan and cook for about 2 minutes until opaque. Remove and allow to cool.
4 If using fresh pasta, roll out using a pasta machine if possible, then shape into quills (see page 12).
5 Cook the pasta in a large pan of boiling salted water until *al dente*; fresh pasta will only take about 3 minutes. Drain and cool.
6 Gently toss the pasta with the fennel, squid and tomato salsa. Chill until required. Serve garnished with fennel and lemon wedges.

Smoked Mussel and Pasta Salad

Serves 4
Preparation 15 minutes
Cooking 20 minutes
660 calories per serving

Illustrated opposite

An unusual dressing of puréed roasted pepper, olive oil and garlic gives this pasta salad a wonderful flavour, which is further enhanced by the smokey mussels and grilled salad onions. If possible, make the salad in advance to allow the flavours time to mature, but add the avocado just before serving.

2 red peppers, cored, seeded and quartered
8 salad onions, peeled and quartered
90 ml (3 fl oz) olive oil
1 garlic clove, peeled and roughly chopped
10 ml (2 tsp) red wine vinegar
salt and pepper
350 g (12 oz) dried pasta shapes, such as shells, tubes or bows

125 g (4 oz) fresh or frozen peas
two 105 g (3½ oz) cans smoked mussels, drained
30 ml (2 tbsp) chopped fresh parsley
1 avocado, peeled, stoned and cut into chunks
parsley sprigs, to garnish

1 Preheat the grill. Place the quartered peppers, skin-side up, and onions in the grill pan and drizzle with 15 ml (1 tbsp) olive oil. Grill until the pepper skins are charred and the onions are nicely browned. (You may need to remove the onions before the peppers.) Place the peppers in a bowl, cover and leave until cool enough to handle (the steam created will help to loosen the skins).
2 Peel the peppers and place half in a blender or food processor with the remaining oil, garlic and vinegar. Work to a purée, and add seasoning to taste.
3 Cook the pasta in a large pan of boiling salted water until *al dente*, adding the peas about 5 minutes before the end of the cooking time. Drain the cooked pasta and peas, refresh under cold running water and drain thoroughly.
4 Transfer the pasta and peas to a large bowl, add the pepper dressing and

toss well. Cut the remaining pepper into strips, and add to the salad with the grilled onions, mussels, chopped parsley and avocado. Toss gently to combine all the ingredients and check the seasoning. Serve garnished with parsley.

NOTE: Canned smoked mussels are available from large supermarkets and delicatessens. Smoked oysters are a delicious alternative.

Harlequin Pepper, Olive and Pasta Salad

Serves 4
Preparation 20 minutes
Cooking About 35 minutes
640 calories per serving

This mouth-watering warm salad is full of good, strong Mediterranean flavours. The piquant dressing uses two whole bulbs of roasted garlic which may sound excessive, but garlic, when roasted, loses its pungency and becomes deliciously sweet and creamy. The salad is equally good served cold.

1 red pepper
1 yellow pepper
1 green pepper
30 ml (2 tbsp) olive oil
1 large red onion, peeled and finely sliced
2 sticks celery, peeled and finely diced
2 tomatoes, seeded and finely diced
¼-½ teaspoon chilli powder (optional)
225 g (8 oz) pitted black olives, halved
75 g (3 oz) capers in wine vinegar, rinsed and drained

4 canned anchovies in oil, drained and cut into thin strips (optional)
250 g (9 oz) fresh tagliatelle
salt and pepper

DRESSING
2 whole garlic bulbs
a little oil, for brushing
2 tomatoes, skinned, seeded and chopped
90 ml (6 tbsp) olive oil
30 ml (2 tbsp) red wine vinegar

TO GARNISH
chopped oregano or coriander

1 Preheat the oven to 200°C (400°F) Mark 6. Put the whole peppers and garlic bulbs (for the dressing) on a baking sheet and brush the garlic with a little oil. Bake in the oven for about 25 minutes or until quite soft. Set aside the garlic. Place the peppers in a covered bowl and leave until cool enough to handle. Peel away the skins, remove the core and seeds, and dice the flesh.

2 Heat the oil in a heavy-based frying pan, add the onion and celery, cover and cook gently for 10 minutes until softened, but not coloured.

3 Meanwhile, combine the diced peppers, tomatoes, chilli powder if using, olives, capers and anchovies in a bowl.

4 To make the dressing, snip the tips off the roasted garlic bulbs and squeeze the flesh into a blender or food processor. Add the remaining ingredients, season with salt and pepper to taste and work until smooth.

5 Cook the pasta in a large saucepan of boiling salted water until *al dente*.

6 Meanwhile, add the pepper and olive mixture to the onion and celery. Warm through over a low heat, stir in the dressing and warm gently.

7 Drain the pasta and toss with the pepper and olive salsa. Check the seasoning. Serve immediately, sprinkled with oregano or coriander.

Warm Bean and Pasta Salad with Herb Dressing

Serves 6
Preparation 10 minutes
Cooking About 10 minutes
630 calories per serving

15 ml (1 tbsp) olive oil
1 large garlic clove, peeled and crushed
425 g (15 oz) can cannellini beans, rinsed and drained
425 g (15 oz) can black eye beans, rinsed and drained
425 g (15 oz) can butter beans, rinsed and drained
30 ml (2 tbsp) sherry
30 ml (2 tbsp) white wine vinegar
250 g (8 oz) pasta shells
salt and pepper

DRESSING
2 large shallots or ½ small onion, peeled and roughly chopped
60 ml (4 tbsp) ground almonds
1 garlic clove, peeled and quartered
15 ml (1 tbsp) sherry
about 60 ml (4 tbsp) flat-leaved parsley
150 ml (¼ pint) olive oil

TO SERVE
salad leaves
parsley sprigs, to garnish

1 Put the ingredients for the dressing into a blender or a food processor and process briefly until evenly well blended, but still retaining some texture.

2 Heat the oil in a large sauté pan over a moderate heat, add the garlic and fry for 1 minute. Add the beans and toss well.

3 Pour in the sherry and vinegar and cook for a further 3 minutes. Remove from the heat and allow to cool.

4 Cook the pasta in a large pan of boiling salted water until *al dente*. Drain and refresh in a bowl of cold water; drain thoroughly.

5 Put the beans and pasta into a large bowl, pour over the dressing and toss thoroughly. Serve on a bed of salad leaves garnished with parsley.

VARIATIONS
Replace one or two of the bean varieties with freshly cooked broad beans or French beans, cut into short lengths.

Mediterranean Pasta Salad

Serves 4
Preparation 15 minutes, plus standing
Cooking About 10 minutes
415 calories per serving

The flavours of the Mediterranean are captured in this salad of pasta, sun-dried tomatoes, black olives, basil leaves, shredded spring onions and cherry tomatoes. Any pasta shapes can be used; if preferred use tricolore pasta – a mixture of spinach, tomato and plain pasta.

175 g (6 oz) dried pasta shapes
15 ml (1 tbsp) extra-virgin olive oil
4 sun-dried tomatoes in oil, drained and sliced
225 g (8 oz) cherry tomatoes, halved
4-6 spring onions, trimmed and shredded
about 8-12 black olives
8-12 basil leaves, torn

DRESSING
2 sun-dried tomatoes in oil, drained
30 ml (2 tbsp) oil (from the sun-dried tomato jar)
30 ml (2 tbsp) red wine vinegar
1 garlic clove, peeled
15 ml (1 tbsp) tomato purée
pinch of sugar (optional)
coarse sea salt and pepper
30 ml (2 tbsp) extra-virgin olive oil

1 Cook the pasta in a large pan of boiling salted water until *al dente*. Drain in a colander, then refresh under cold running water. Drain thoroughly and transfer to a large bowl. Stir in 15 ml (1 tbsp) olive oil to prevent the pasta from sticking together.

2 Add the sun-dried and cherry tomatoes, spring onions, olives and basil, and toss to mix.

3 To make the dressing, put the sun-dried tomatoes and oil, vinegar, garlic and tomato purée in a blender or food processor. Add the sugar if using, and salt and pepper. With the motor running, pour the olive oil through the feeder tube and process briefly to make a fairly thick dressing.

4 Pour the dressing over the pasta and toss well. Cover and leave to stand to allow the flavours to mingle for 1-2 hours before serving if possible.

VARIATION
Toss cubes of mature Cheddar cheese into the salad and serve with wholemeal bread and a leafy green salad for a main course.

Gingered Prawn and Lasagnette Salad

Serves 4
Preparation 20 minutes
Cooking 15 minutes
465 calories per serving

Illustrated opposite

Flash-fried vegetables and succulent prawns are tossed with curly pasta in an oriental-style dressing for this attractive main meal salad. Any other plain pasta shapes can be used instead of the lasagnette.

450 g (1 lb) large raw prawns in shells (see note)
225 g (8 oz) fresh or dried lasagnette
salt and pepper
30 ml (2 tbsp) oil
225 g (8 oz) baby carrots, halved lengthwise
125 g (4 oz) baby courgettes, halved lengthwise
1 bunch spring onions, trimmed and sliced
4 garlic cloves, peeled and thinly sliced

1 red chilli, seeded and chopped
175 g (6 oz) Chinese leaves, shredded
60 ml (4 tbsp) roughly chopped fresh parsley or coriander

DRESSING
1 piece preserved stem ginger, finely chopped, plus 30 ml (2 tbsp) syrup from the jar
15 ml (1 tbsp) soy sauce
15 ml (1 tbsp) sesame oil

TO GARNISH
30 ml (2 tbsp) sesame seeds, toasted

1 Peel the prawns and butterfly, by snipping each one lengthwise almost in half from head to tail, leaving the tail end intact; set aside.
2 For the dressing, combine the ginger and syrup, soy sauce and sesame oil.
3 Cook the pasta in a large pan of boiling salted water until *al dente*. Drain and place in a bowl. Add the dressing and toss to coat evenly.
4 Heat the oil in a large frying pan. Add the carrots and courgettes and fry very quickly over a high heat until lightly charred. Remove with a slotted spoon and set aside. Add the spring onions, garlic, chilli, Chinese leaves and prawns. Fry quickly until the prawns are cooked and the leaves are just wilted.
5 Add all the vegetables to the pasta with the parsley or coriander, and a little seasoning. Serve warm, scattered with toasted sesame seeds.

VARIATION
Instead of raw prawns, use 350 g (12 oz) cooked peeled prawns. Omit stage 1. Add the prawns at the end of stage 4 and heat through briefly.

Prawn and Glass Noodle Salad

Serves 4
Preparation 15 minutes
Cooking 1 minute
170 calories per serving

Glass or cellophane noodles have a transparent quality, which makes them an attractive and unusual addition to a salad. Serve this salad as a starter, or light lunch.

75 g (3 oz) shiitake mushrooms, finely sliced
50 g (2 oz) glass noodles
1 large carrot, peeled and cut into julienne strips
1 large courgette, cut into julienne strips
12 large cooked shelled prawns

DRESSING
2 garlic cloves, peeled and crushed

15 ml (1 tbsp) light soy sauce
30 ml (2 tbsp) sugar
15 ml (1 tbsp) wine vinegar
15 ml (1 tbsp) sesame oil
1 red chilli, seeded and finely shredded

TO GARNISH
15 ml (1 tbsp) toasted sesame seeds
30 ml (2 tbsp) chopped coriander

1 First make the dressing: mix all of the ingredients together in a small bowl. Add the mushrooms to the dressing and toss well.
2 Cut the noodles into 10 cm (4 inch) lengths. Cook in boiling water for 1 minute or according to packet instructions. Drain thoroughly and put in a bowl.
3 Add the mushrooms with the dressing, carrot, courgette and prawns to the noodles. Toss well and serve warm, sprinkled with the sesame seeds and coriander.

Tomato, Red Onion, Avocado and Pappardelle Salad

Serves 4
Preparation 20 minutes, plus pasta
Cooking 2-4 minutes
530 calories per serving

This colourful, refreshing salad is quickly assembled. If preferred, use dried pasta shapes, such as twists or shells, rather than fresh pappardelle.

250 g (9 oz) fresh sun-dried tomato pappardelle (see page 11)

salt and pepper

4 large ripe tomatoes, skinned, quartered and diced

1 medium red onion, peeled and finely diced

75 g (3 oz) sun-dried tomatoes in oil, drained and diced

1 plump red chilli, seeded and finely diced

2 avocados, peeled and diced

60 ml (4 tbsp) coarsely chopped fresh coriander leaves

DRESSING
45 ml (3 tbsp) light soy sauce
30 ml (2 tbsp) sesame oil
juice of 1 lime
7.5-10 ml (1½-2 tsp) sugar, or to taste
white pepper

1 Cook the pasta in a large saucepan of boiling salted water until *al dente*; freshly made pappardelle will take about 2 minutes; bought fresh pasta about 3-4 minutes.

2 Meanwhile, for the dressing, put the soy sauce, sesame oil, lime juice, sugar and a little pepper in a small screw-topped jar and shake vigorously to blend.

3 Drain the pasta and refresh in a bowl of very cold, salted water until ready to use. Drain thoroughly and place in a large bowl with the tomatoes, onion, sun-dried tomatoes, chilli, avocados and coriander. Pour over the dressing and toss carefully. Check the seasoning and serve at once.

Sunshine Pasta Salad

Serves 4
Preparation 15 minutes
Cooking 10 minutes
460 calories per serving

A colourful, crunchy salad – ideal to serve during the summer months, when tomatoes are flavourful.

175 g (6 oz) dried pasta, such as orecchiette or shells

salt and pepper

450 g (1 lb) ripe tomatoes, skinned, seeded and cut into strips

175 g (6 oz) piece cucumber, halved lengthwise, seeded and sliced

175 g (6 oz) celery sticks, sliced

50 g (2 oz) pitted black olives, halved

DRESSING
15 ml (1 tbsp) wine vinegar
5 ml (1 tsp) Dijon mustard
120 ml (8 tbsp) olive oil
30 ml (2 tbsp) sun-dried tomato paste
10 ml (2 tsp) paprika
1 garlic clove, peeled

TO GARNISH
handful of fresh basil leaves

1 To make the dressing, blend the ingredients together in a food processor until smooth.

2 Cook the pasta in a large pan of boiling salted water until *al dente*. Drain and toss with the dressing. Cover and set aside to cool.

3 Add the tomatoes, cucumber, celery and olives to the cooled pasta and season with salt and papper to taste. Serve topped with basil leaves.

INDEX